PICTURE THESE

SAT *

WORDS!

FOURTH EDITION

ALL THE VOCABULARY YOU NEED TO SUCCEED ON THE SAT

Philip Geer and Susan Geer
Illustrated by Bob Bourdeaux

ABOUT THE AUTHORS

PHILIP GEER has taught English language and literature for many years and is the author of a number of test preparation books, including *6 SAT Practice Tests*, *Essential Words for the GRE*, and *GRE Verbal Workbook*, all published by Barron's.

SUSAN GEER is the director of Mentaurs Educational Consultants, which prepares students for various tests of verbal and writing ability, including the SAT and the GRE. She has been helping students improve their verbal skills for over thirty years.

All inquiries should be addressed to:
Barron's Educational Series, Inc.
250 Wireless Boulevard
Hauppauge, New York 11788
www.barronseduc.com

ISBN: 978-1-4380-1077-9

Library of Congress Control Number: 2017962250

PRINTED IN CANADA

9 8 7 6 5 4 3 2 1

CONTENTS

INTRODUCTION / v

Vocabulary Is Still Important / v
Words in Context Are Tested Regularly / v
High-Frequency SAT Words / vi
High-Frequency Words on the Redesigned SAT / vi
How the SUPER-MNEMONICS Method Works / vii
Study Plan / x
Have Fun As You Learn / x

MEET THE STARS / xi
Meet the Stars Quiz / 16

UNIT 1 / 19
Quiz 1 / 31

UNIT 2 / 33
Quiz 2 / 45

UNIT 3 / 47
Quiz 3 / 59

UNIT 4 / 61
Quiz 4 / 73

UNIT 5 / 75
Quiz 5 / 87

UNIT 6 / 89
Quiz 6 / 101

UNIT 7 / 103
Quiz 7 / 115

UNIT 8 / 117
Quiz 8 / 129

UNIT 9 / 131
Quiz 9 / 143

UNIT 10 / 145
Quiz 10 / 157

UNIT 11 / 159
Quiz 11 / 171

UNIT 12 / 173
Quiz 12 / 185

UNIT 13 / 187
Quiz 13 / 199

UNIT 14 / 201
Quiz 14 / 213

UNIT 15 / 215
Quiz 15 / 227

UNIT 16 / 229
Quiz 16 / 241

UNIT 17 / 243
Quiz 17 / 255

UNIT 18 / 257
Quiz 18 / 269

UNIT 19 / 271
Quiz 19 / 283

UNIT 20 / 285
Quiz 20 / 297

UNIT 21 / 299
Quiz 21 / 311

UNIT 22 / 313
Quiz 22 / 325

UNIT 23 / 327
Quiz 23 / 339

UNIT 24 / 341
Quiz 24 / 353

UNIT 25 / 355
Quiz 25 / 367

Answers / 369

INTRODUCTION

VOCABULARY IS STILL IMPORTANT

Some students believe that a strong vocabulary is not necessary to do well on the redesigned SAT. This is not true. Although vocabulary is no longer tested directly in sentence completion questions, difficult words still appear regularly in the passages and questions of the Reading Test, as well as in the passages and questions of the Writing and Language Test. To truly understand what you are reading, you must understand *all* the words. While the SAT no longer tests really advanced words—like *refractory, execrable,* or *insouciant,* for example—the makers of the test, the College Board, say that the redesigned test contains "vocabulary you'll use long after test day." By this they mean fairly difficult words that are regularly used in formal discourse by educated readers and writers— the novelists, critics, scientists, artists, philosophers, and others who write the passages that the College Board uses in its test. These are words like *conventional, elaborate,* and *subscribe,* and they appear regularly on the SAT. *Picture These SAT Words* will teach you 315 of the most important of these words so that you'll have a powerful arsenal of words at your disposal, not only to do well on the SAT, but also to use throughout your entire academic career.

WORDS IN CONTEXT ARE TESTED REGULARLY

The other major change related to vocabulary on the redesigned SAT is that words are now often tested *in context*. In fact, this skill is so important that a "Words in Context" subscore is reported with your SAT score. Therefore, you must be able to determine which—among several possible meanings a word can have—is the meaning the word has in a particular phrase or sentence.

In this edition of *Picture These SAT Words*, illustrative sentences for each word will show how that word can be used in a range of situations. This will not only familiarize you with the ways the word can be used, but it will also sharpen your skills in determining the meaning of words in context.

HIGH-FREQUENCY SAT WORDS

Let's look at the following list of some of the words that appeared in recent practice tests for the redesigned SAT, as published by the College Board. How many of these words do you know? Words that appear in bold are words that have appeared with very high frequency on SAT tests over the years and continue to appear with very high frequency on the redesigned SAT. If you are like most students, you will probably know some of them, while others may look familiar but you may not be sure what they mean.

HIGH-FREQUENCY WORDS ON THE REDESIGNED SAT

abstract	**cynical**	**melancholy**
adversary	**depict**	mitigate
advocate	**deterrent**	**mundane**
aesthetic	**dilemma**	nurture
aggregate	diligence	**obscure**
altruism	**discern**	**obsolete**
ambiguous	**disdain**	**ornate**
ambivalence	disparity	**parody**
analogous	divergent	perpetuate
anomaly	**diversity**	**phenomena**
articulate	document	**polarize**
aspire	egotism	**pretentious**
attribute	**elaborate**	**proliferate**
austere	**emit**	**quandary**
authoritarian	ephemeral	repel
autonomous	**evoke**	**rhetoric**
beguile	exalt	**satirical**
beneficial	explicit	scrutinize
benevolent	facilitate	**stoic**
bolster	**feasible**	**subscribe**
calculated	**inadvertent**	**substantial**
colloquial	**indifference**	superficial
compile	**innovation**	terrestrial
comprehensive	**ironic**	trifling
consequence	**jaded**	**undermine**
conventional	lament	

The good news is that 315 important words you need to know to do well on the SAT, including many of these "High-Frequency Words on the Redesigned SAT," can be learned by using this book. *Picture These SAT Words!* will teach you all the words quickly and efficiently. Furthermore, it will really *teach* you the words—not just acquaint you with them, which is what most vocabulary books do. This is because this book uses a totally new method—SUPER-MNEMONICS—to fix each word and its meaning permanently in your memory. After you have learned the 315 words in this book, you won't ever forget them. You'll have a solid base of advanced, college-level vocabulary that you will be able to rely on to get a great score on the SAT Reading Test and the Writing and Language Test. You will also have a great foundation of important words for your further studies. New to this edition is the bonus unit entitled *Meet the Stars*. It will introduce you to 15 of the most frequently occurring words in recent tests of the redesigned SAT.

HOW THE SUPER-MNEMONICS METHOD WORKS

A mnemonic is "a short rhyme, phrase, or other mental technique for making information easier to memorize" (Encarta Dictionary). There are many different types of mnemonics. Schoolchildren are taught catchy rhymes to remember dates, like that of Columbus' discovery of America:

> In fourteen hundred and ninety-two,
> Columbus sailed the ocean blue.

Another type of mnemonic is the acronym—a word formed from the initial letters of a name. Acronyms are helpful in remembering lists. Science students are taught to recall the order of the seven colors visible within the spectrum of light by the acronym ROY G. BIV—*R*ed, *O*range, *Y*ellow, *G*reen, *B*lue, *I*ndigo, *V*iolet. ROY G. BIV is a simple mnemonic that works for something straightforward.

To memorize SAT words, however, a different kind of mnemonic is needed—a super-mnemonic—that will teach not only the SAT word but also its meaning.

SUPER-MNEMONICS makes learning difficult words easy. It is fast, simple, and efficient. If you don't have much time left before the test, you need to improve your vocabulary fast. It makes more sense to learn 315 words well than to waste time trying to memorize long lists of words.

SUPER-MNEMONICS is a totally new method of vocabulary building. It links the *sound* of each word to an unforgettable *picture* that illustrates the meaning of the word. SUPER-MNEMONICS is a fast and effective way to learn.

Three easy steps fix each SAT word and definition permanently in your memory.

1. Let's take the word heresy. Sound it out. Say, "HAIR uh see."

2. Read the sound link

Picture this:
Hair-a-Sea

3. Look at the picture and its funny caption on the next page. An unforgettable pictorial link is created in your memory between the word heresy and its meaning. Whenever you sound out the word heresy, you'll connect it with its sound link *Hair-a-Sea* and the picture will appear in your mind, telling you its meaning.

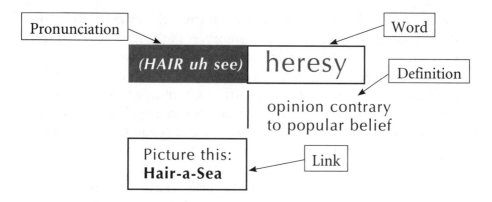

In the little village of *Hair-a-Sea*
it's *heresy* not to have hair.

Everyone in this little village by the sea has a long mane of hair, except for one bald man. This bald man believes "It's OK NOT to have hair," as it says on his shirt. He is being chased out of Hair-a-Sea by the villagers because he has committed the heresy of having an opinion contrary to theirs.

By following these three easy steps, you'll learn each of the words in this book. After a word is fixed in your memory, read the sentences that show how it can be used. This will help you understand that word better when it appears on the SAT. To make certain that you've learned the words in each unit, be sure to do the exercises after each unit. "Memory Check" makes sure that you can relate the word to its meaning. "Showtime" is your chance to show that you've learned the words and that you can use them in sentences like the ones on the actual SAT.

The words in *Picture These SAT Words!* appear regularly not only on the SAT, but on other major tests, such as the GRE and the GMAT. SUPER-MNEMONICS makes the words unforgettable, so the 315 words you've learned to get a good SAT score will also help you later on when you have to take similar tests. *Picture These SAT Words!* is also an excellent book for preparing for the PSAT, the ACT, the SSAT/ISEE, and the GED.

STUDY PLAN

How you use this book depends on how much time you have before the test. If, for example, you only have a week to go before the test, you could learn sixty-three words a day for five days. That's all 315 words in this book. And you'll still have your weekend free. If you have a month or so, your pace can be more leisurely. You can do one unit a day. In twenty-six days you'll have memorized the meanings of all 315 words in *Picture These SAT Words!*

HAVE FUN AS YOU LEARN

One more thing—*Picture These SAT Words!* is fun! You'll travel to strange new worlds: Paw City, a town of "well-pawed" folks, and A Duel Nation, where dueling is a national obsession. You'll meet a cast of fascinating characters, like Bill Reese, the handsome company rep; dill gents, pickled Southern gentlemen; satirical satyrs, ready to party; and the girl with the vapor eyes (watch out or she'll vaporize you!). So, you'll have plenty of fun as you're learning these SAT words. Start picturing these SAT words now to build your vocabulary and get a great score on the SAT.

Have fun learning!

Philip Geer and Susan Geer

MEET THE STARS

After thoroughly researching published tests of the redesigned SAT, 15 words stood out and are thus critical for you to know. These words repeatedly appeared on the SAT Reading Test and the Writing and Language Test. Since they have been used so frequently on the actual exam, we like to call them our "shining stars." Now, it's time for you to get to know them.

(kun VEN shun ul)	conventional

customary; conforming to accepted standards

Picture this:
convention all

At a *convention*, *all* must wear *conventional* suits.

- The *conventional* wedding ceremony that is so popular in modern America is modeled on the wedding ceremonies of European royalty of the nineteenth century.

- The new book calls *conventional* thinking on the issue into question.

- The critic suggested that the writer use more *conventional* phraseology in his next book.

cynical

(SIN ih kul)

skeptical or distrustful
of others' motives

Picture this:
Cyn Nickel

Cynthia Nickel (*Cyn Nickel* for short)
is a very *cynical* nickel.

■ Despite her thirty years as a prosecutor, Alicia refused to become *cynical* about human nature.

■ Some critics of the latest Broadway hit say that it promotes a *cynical* attitude toward other people.

■ A rather *cynical* Persian proverb says, "Trust in God, but tie your camel."

(dih LEM ah)	dilemma

a perplexing
situation

Picture this:
Dill Emma

I can't decide which jar to jump into.
My reputation is at stake,
so I'd better pick
the right one.
But they all look so good!

Dill Emma

Jeremy's Dills

Rocky's Gourmet Dills

Diane's Finest Dills

What a *dilemma* for poor *Dill Emma*!

■ A common *dilemma* faced by students is whether to pursue a field that interests them or one that has good employment prospects.

■ In the Vietnam War era, many young men faced a *dilemma*: allow themselves to be drafted to fight in a war they didn't believe in or refuse to obey the law and face the legal consequences.

■ Emily faces a *dilemma*: she's been accepted by both Harvard and Yale and she'd love to attend either one.

3

discern

to perceive something

Picture this:
dis urn

On *dis urn*, I *discern* the owl of the goddess Athena.

■ The rings of Saturn can be *discerned* with the use of a telescope.

■ Older people sometimes have difficulty *discerning* the difference between the number zero and the letter "O" on a computer screen.

■ The soldier standing guard *discerned* enemy soldiers advancing on his camp.

diversity

variety

Picture this:
Diverse City

A *diversity* of housing styles in *Diverse City*.

■ The college's admission policy is to seek a wide *diversity* of students.

■ Charles Darwin marveled at the *diversity* of life on Earth produced by evolution.

■ Dieticians recommend eating a *diversity* of foods to promote good health.

elaborate

to add details

Picture this:
Eel Lab bore 8

Eel Lab bore 8 eels who liked to *elaborate* on eel life.

- The essay would have been better if the writer had *elaborated* on his argument.

- The police officer asked the witness to *elaborate* on her account of the traffic accident.

- The candidate for political office chose not to *elaborate* on his proposal because he was afraid that doing so would provide details for his opponent to attack.

(JAY did)	jaded

wearied; tired or bored
by excess or overuse

Picture this:
Jade Ed

Jade Ed was *jaded* as a result of
all the jade he was wearing.

■ Since his appetite was *jaded* due to years of fine dining,
Luke decided to eat at a diner for a change.

■ Because teachers often become *jaded* after years of teaching,
many schools grant teachers long-term service leave after a set
number of years.

■ His sad story left me *jaded* and depressed.

melancholy

(MEL uhn kahl ee)

sad; depressed

Picture this:
Melon Collie

A *melancholy Melon Collie* guards the watermelons.

■ It is a *melancholy* fact that wars still occur regularly around the world.

■ The deaths in the family created a *melancholy* atmosphere in the house.

■ Some religions teach that death, far from being something to be *melancholy* about, is a return to a higher form of existence.

obsolete

no longer used;
outmoded in design,
style, or construction

Picture this:
Ob sole eat

Ob, *sole eat* atop an *obsolete* Model T.

■ One fashion writer stated that the miniskirt is now *obsolete*.

■ Some school teachers consider chalkboards to be *obsolete*, but others believe they still have a place in the classroom.

■ Some experts predict that printed books will one day become *obsolete*.

polarize

(POH luh rize)

to tend toward opposite extremes; to divide into opposing groups

Picture this:
polar rise

Polar bears *polarized* on a *polar rise*.

■ During the Cold War era, much of the world was *polarized*, with many countries in the Soviet Bloc and many others in a group led by the United States.

■ The survey shows that people are *polarized* on the question of whether there is too much violence depicted on television.

■ It has become common to describe America as *polarized* into "red" (Republican) states and "blue" (Democrat) states.

quandary

state of uncertainty;
dilemma

Picture this:
Kwan Dairy

A *quandary* took place at *Kwan Dairy*.

■ Many young working men and women face a *quandary* when they start a family—keep working to earn money or quit their job to give more attention to their children.

■ The lost hiker was in a *quandary*: continue walking or stop and wait for rescue.

■ Because he loves both lamb chops and steak, Tom was in a *quandary* about what to have for dinner.

rhetoric

(RET er ik)

persuasive use of language;
persuasive language
that lacks sincerity or
meaningful content

Picture this:
Rhet or Rick

For *rhetoric*, choose *Rhet or Rick*.
Either one will do the trick.

■ A popular phrase used by politicians to criticize their opponents' speeches is "empty *rhetoric*."

■ The essay required students to analyze the *rhetoric* of a prose passage.

■ A good knowledge of *rhetoric* allows one to logically examine a writer's argument and analyze its strengths and weaknesses.

(STOH ik)	stoic

indifferent to or unaffected
by pleasure or pain

Picture this:
Stowe Wick

Stoic customers stuck at the
Stowe Wick in Stowe, Vermont.

■ The religion encourages in its adherents a *stoic*
  acceptance of God's will.

■ The leader urged the people to be *stoic* and endure the period
  of austerity.

■ Even after learning that he won the lottery, Evan's
  expression remained *stoic*.

subscribe

(suhb SKRIBE)

to agree; to sanction

Picture this:
sub scribe

The *sub scribe subscribes* to traditional methods.

■ Americans *subscribe* to the view that everyone is equal before the law.

■ The religion requires its followers to *subscribe* fully to its dogma.

■ We prefer to *subscribe* to an alternative view on that issue.

substantial

of ample size, amount, or quantity

Picture this:
Sub Stan shall

Sub Stan shall make us a *substantial* sub sandwich.

- Tom's college tuition represents a *substantial* portion of his family's budget.

- The newspaper editorial praised the governor for "*substantial* progress" in reducing the state's budget deficit.

- Although support for the proposal is far from unanimous, a *substantial* section of the population favors it.

Memory Check—Meet the Stars
Match each word and its link to the corresponding definition.

dilemma
1. **Dill Emma** _d_

diversity
2. **Diverse City** _a_

elaborate
3. **Eel Lab bore 8** _g_

jaded
4. **Jade Ed** _e_

melancholy
5. **Melon Collie** _c_

polarize
6. **polar rise** _b_

rhetoric
7. **Rhet or Rick** _f_

a. variety
b. to divide into opposing groups
c. sad; depressed
d. a perplexing situation
e. wearied; tired or bored by excess or overuse

f. persuasive use of language; persuasive language that lacks sincerity or meaningful content
g. to add details

Showtime—Meet the Stars
Fill in the blanks in the following sentences with the word or set of words that best fits the meaning of the sentence as a whole.

1. After repeatedly being deceived by people, Judy became _____.
   a. obsolete   b. substantial   c. beneficial   d. thoughtful   (e.) cynical

2. The horse-drawn carriage is _____ means of transportation in developed countries.
   a. a cynical   b. a stoic   (c.) an obsolete   d. a rapid   e. a melancholy

3. We could barely _____ the figure coming toward us in the thick fog.
   a. emit   b. polarize   c. deduce   (d.) discern   e. elaborate

4. The leader of the extremely poor country faced _____: spend the little money available on education or on health care.
   a. an opponent   b. a diversity   c. an advantage
   d. rhetoric   (e.) a quandary

16

5. Red is the color _____ used in traffic lights to indicate that a motorist must stop.

a. stoically   b. conventionally   c. rhetorically
d. variously   e. cynically

6. The commander asked the soldiers to try to be _____ about their fate in the upcoming battle.

a. beneficial   b. jaded   c. stoic   d. polarized   e. substantial

7. Scientists _____ the view that the universe is governed by laws of nature that can be discovered by careful observation.

a. precede   b. subscribe to   c. repel   d. disguise   e. polarize

8. The grand jury found the evidence to be _____ enough to indict the accused.

a. melancholy   b. jaded   c. cynical   d. compact   e. substantial

abstemious

eating and drinking in
moderation; restricted to
bare necessities

Picture this:
Ab's steamy us

UNIT 1

It's **bread and water** for this family from now on!

VISA $800
Ice cream $200

Pizza $100

AB

Ab's steamy with *us* when
he tells us to be *abstemious*.

■ After feasting on Thanksgiving Day, I became *abstemious*
for a few days, so I lost some of the weight I had put on.

■ Medical experts say that a fairly *abstemious* lifestyle is
advisable for good health.

■ Models often must be *abstemious* in order to avoid
gaining weight.

abstract

not concrete; theoretical

Picture this:
Ab's tract*

Ab's grand tract of land

Ab, stop daydreaming!

Ab's tract is only *abstract*.

■ The idea of infinity is an *abstract* concept that people have difficulty imagining.

■ When discussing *abstract* ideas, such as truth, justice, and freedom, in an essay, you should give concrete examples to illustrate your argument.

■ We have been discussing the problem in an *abstract* manner, but we must eventually consider how to solve it in practical terms.

* A *tract* is an area of land.

abstruse

difficult to
understand

Picture this:
Ab's truce

Ab's truce is too ***abstruse*** for the
ducks and their killer moose.

■ Writers who are *abstruse* seldom are really popular.

■ Many people find higher mathematics to be an *abstruse* subject.

■ The astronomer Carl Sagan had a gift for making the *abstruse* areas of his field understandable to the layperson.

acclaim

(uh KLAYM)

applaud; announce
with great approval

Picture this:
a claim

They *acclaim* him for staking
a claim to her heart.

■ Thomas A. Edison was *acclaimed* around the world for his
many useful inventions.

■ Often it takes a talented new author many years to win the
acclaim of readers and critics.

■ The principal *acclaimed* the winner of the Best Student of
the Year award and then gave him a prize.

accolade

(AK kuh layd)

award of merit

Picture this:
a coal aide

*A **coal aide*** receives an ***accolade**.*

■ A Pulitzer Prize is one of the highest *accolades* that a writer can receive.

■ Some writers achieve great popularity but never win *accolades* from literary critics.

■ Ms. Miller, this year's Teacher of the Year, says she works not for *accolades* but for the benefit of her students.

acknowledge *(ak NAHL ij)*

recognize;
admit

Picture this:
knowledge

They always *acknowledge* her *knowledge*.

■ *Acknowledging* our shortcomings is the first step to changing ourselves for the better.

■ Many writers *acknowledge* the help that they've received in writing a book on a special dedication page.

■ The company *acknowledged* Mr. Smith's many years of service with a set of golf clubs.

(ak wee ES)	acquiesce

agree without
protesting

Picture this:
Aqua S

"The *Aqua S* pool is top of the line!
You *will* *acquiesce* to purchasing it!"

■ Soldiers are expected to *acquiesce* to the orders of their
superior officers.

■ Reluctantly, Linda *acquiesced* to Jim's wishes and went to
the football game with him; to her surprise, she enjoyed it.

■ The company *acquiesced* to the union's demands after
a twelve-week strike nearly bankrupted the business.

adulation

(aj uh LAY shun)

flattery;
admiration

Picture this:
a duel nation

Ye Old Duel Inn

MEN AT ARMS

In *a duel nation*, duelers receive *adulation*.

■ Rock stars often receive widespread *adulation* for a short period of time.

■ On some college campuses, there are movements to place less stress on intercollegiate athletics so that good students receive as much *adulation* as good athletes.

■ After World War II, General Dwight D. Eisenhower received so much *adulation* for leading the Allies to victory that it helped him be elected president of the United States.

adversary

opponent

Picture this:
add verse* sari

Her *adversary* likes to *add verse* to her *sari*.

■ Before committing her country to war, a wise leader carefully sizes up the strength of the possible *adversary*.

■ During World War II, Japan found that the United States was a more powerful *adversary* than it had thought the U.S. would be.

■ For many years, Muhammad Ali and Joe Frazier were regular *adversaries* in the boxing ring, fighting for the heavyweight championship of the world.

* *Verse* is poetry.

adversity

(ad VUR sih tee)

poverty; misfortune

Picture this:
Adverse City

Adversity exists in *Adverse City*.

■ Some people believe that *adversity* improves character, making one a stronger and more understanding person.

■ During a war, civilians as well as soldiers usually experience *adversity*.

■ The stoic philosophers of ancient Greece believed that facing *adversity* calmly is a great virtue.

advocate

verb: urge; plead for

noun: one who argues in favor of something

Picture this:
ad vote Kate

In an *ad vote*, *Kate advocates* vegetable rights.

■ The government of the United States *advocates* democracy as the best political system for all countries.

■ People who *advocate* increased immigration to Australia argue that the country has enough resources to support far more people than it does now.

■ The *advocates* of a higher minimum wage support their case by saying that it is nearly impossible for a person to survive on the present minimum wage.

aesthetic

pertaining to
art or beauty

Picture this:
S that tick

Oh beautiful *S*! *That tick*
tickles the *aesthetic* sense!

- To be successful, an interior decorator needs to have a well-developed *aesthetic* sense.

- A well-designed house combines practical and *aesthetic* elements so that it is pleasing both to live in and to look at.

- *Aesthetics* is a branch of philosophy that studies such questions as what makes something beautiful.

Memory Check 1

Match each word and its link to the corresponding definition.

acknowledge
1. **knowledge** __

adversity
2. **Adverse City** __

abstract
3. **Ab's tract** __

accolade
4. **a coal aide** __

abstemious
5. **Ab's steamy us** __

abstruse
6. **Ab's truce** __

acclaim
7. **a claim** __

adulation
8. **a duel nation** __

adversary
9. **add verse sari** __

acquiesce
10. **Aqua S** __

aesthetic
11. **S that tick** __

advocate
12. **ad vote Kate** __

a. eating and drinking in moderation
b. agree without protesting
c. plead for
d. applaud; announce with great approval
e. award of merit
f. difficult to understand
g. recognize; admit
h. not concrete
i. pertaining to art or beauty
j. opponent
k. misfortune
l. flattery; admiration

Showtime 1

Fill in the blanks in the following sentences with the word or set of words that best fits the meaning of the sentence as a whole.

1. Sally enjoys visiting museums to look at _____ art, while Peter enjoys going to see realistic art.

   a. interesting   b. abstract   c. abstemious   d. ancient   e. strange

2. My _____ sense is rather limited, so I wasn't confident about expressing my view of the new sculpture.

   a. aesthetic   b. adversity   c. lovely   d. general   e. abstruse

3. The students _____ reforms in the student council that would give them a greater voice in the running of the school, but the principal's reaction to their ideas has been only a vague statement.

   a. advocated   b. acquiesced   c. acknowledged   d. questioned   e. hated

4. John Glenn won nationwide _____ for being the first American to orbit Earth.

    a. justice   b. adversity   c. acclaim   d. joy   e. laughter

5. _____ that you need to lose weight by becoming _____ in what you eat.

    a. Acquiesce.....abstract
    b. Admit.....abstruse
    c. Require.....larger
    d. Show.....regular
    e. Acknowledge.....abstemious

6. My _____ overcame tremendous _____ and defeated me in my best sport, tennis.

    a. friend.....acclaim
    b. adversary.....adversity
    c. accolade.....hardship
    d. classmate.....admiration
    e. enemy.....adulation

7. The rock star was very happy after she won both the _____ of her fans and _____ from music critics for her latest album.

    a. acclaim.....criticism
    b. adulation.....accolades
    c. hatred.....adulation
    d. accolades.....bitterness
    e. attention.....weirdness

8. Although math is a (an) _____ and difficult subject for me, I _____ to my father's order to study it every day.

    a. simple.....acquiesced
    b. abstract.....acclaimed
    c. abstemious.....acknowledged
    d. easy.....agreed
    e. abstruse.....acquiesced

affable

easily approachable;
warmly friendly

Picture this:
Af a bull

UNIT 2

Af, a bull, is so *affable*—his "bull mates"
think he is laughable.

■ Judges at beauty contests often choose one of the
contestants as the most *affable*.

■ People who work in sales are frequently *affable* individuals
who enjoy talking to many types of people.

■ The young teacher was so *affable* that he became his
students' friend but lost their respect.

affirmation

(af ur MAY shun)

assertion; confirmation

Picture this:
a firm mate

A firm mate makes an *affirmation*.

■ Reciting the Pledge of Allegiance is an *affirmation* of our loyalty to our country.

■ Many religions require converts to make an *affirmation* of belief in the teachings of their new religion.

■ The witness nodded in *affirmation* of the judge's statement.

aggregate

total

Picture this:
a gray gate

Beyond *a gray gate* lies the
aggregate wealth of Gray's estate.

■ The Roman Empire was an *aggregate* of many states under the Emperor.

■ The *aggregate* wealth of a country includes the assets of individuals, companies, and other organizations.

■ The *aggregate* strength of the various branches of the U.S. armed services is immense.

alleviate

(uh LEE vee ayt)

relieve;
make more bearable

Picture this:
a leaf he ate

On his plate, there was *a leaf he ate*
to *alleviate* his hunger.

■ The United Nations is working to *alleviate* poverty in
the world.

■ Many people find that exercise is a good way to *alleviate* the
effects of stress.

■ To *alleviate* traffic congestion, cities such as London and
Singapore impose a fee on motorists driving into downtown
areas during busy periods.

aloof

apart;
reserved

Picture this:
a loofa

A loofa acted *aloof*.

■ Shy individuals usually like to remain *aloof* in large gatherings of people.

■ The new student was *aloof* for a few weeks, adjusting to her new classmates.

■ Some managers remain *aloof* from their workers, while others prefer to be "one of the gang."

altruistic

unselfishly generous;
concerned for others

Picture this:
Al True his stick

Al True—his stick selects
those he's *altruistic* to.

■ When one country gives aid to another country, it is generally for reasons that are not entirely *altruistic*.

■ Many people are attracted to teaching for *altruistic* reasons rather than for financial reasons.

■ A mother's love is often cited as an example of *altruism*.

ambiguous

open to more than
one interpretation;
doubtful or uncertain

Picture this:
am big you us

"Who should say 'I *am big*'? *You*? *Us*?
It's not *ambiguous* who is bigger!"

- When writing an essay, try to avoid making *ambiguous* statements.

- Homonyms—words that sound the same but mean different things—are sometimes *ambiguous* when used in speech; *pair/pare/pear* is an example of this.

- The literary value of his best-selling novel is *ambiguous*.

ambivalence

(am BIV uh luns)

the state of having contradictory or conflicting emotional attitudes

Picture this:
am Bev Valence

I really don't like this one . . . *However,* on further consideration . . . And then again . . . the red one *does* look . . . On the other hand . . . . . .

"I *am Bev Valence* and *ambivalence* is my motto."

■ Because he knew that teaching provides a steady income whereas writing usually does not, it was with considerable *ambivalence* that he gave up teaching to become a freelance writer.

■ Joan was attracted to Ted, so she finally agreed to a date with him; however, she did so with some *ambivalence* because of his reputation for being self-centered.

■ Sal was *ambivalent* about whether to try out for the football team or the soccer team because he enjoyed playing each sport equally.

amorphous

formless; lacking
shape or definition

Picture this:
am Orphous

"I *am Orphous*, an *amorphous*
mass of dust and gas."

■ This modern painting is *amorphous*; I can't figure out what
it's supposed to be.

■ The company's plan to expand is at present *amorphous*, but
it should begin to take shape at a series of meetings
next month.

■ This essay is so *amorphous* that it isn't possible to
determine its main argument.

analogous (uh NAL uh gus)

comparable

Picture this:
Anna Low Gus

Anna dating *Low Gus* is *analogous* to
Sammy dating Skinny Russ.

- The heart of an animal or person is *analogous* to a pump.

- An animal's struggle to survive in nature is *analogous* to a company's struggle to survive in the capitalist economic system.

- Businesspeople sometimes make an *analogy* between the hardware of a computer and the "hardware" of a firm—that is, its physical assets, as opposed to its intellectual ones, which are compared to the software used by a computer.

anarchist

a person who seeks to overturn the established government; an advocate of abolishing authority

Picture this:
Anna kissed

Anna kissed a brave young Czar who
saved her from an *anarchist*.

■ Governments regard *anarchists* as dangerous because they represent a threat to the existence of the state.

■ *Anarchists* generally believe that governments infringe on rights that human beings enjoy naturally.

■ Mr. Jones, our principal, seems to regard any student who argues for letting students have a voice in the running of the school as an *anarchist*.

animosity

(an uh MOS i tee)

bitter hostility;
active hatred

Picture this:
Animal City

Animosity happens everywhere in *Animal City*.

■ The once friendly competition between the two rivals for Sue's love has turned into *animosity*.

■ The boxers fighting for the heavyweight championship showed their *animosity* when they shouted angrily at each other at their pre-fight press conference.

■ Some people believe that international sports competitions increase *animosity* among nations, while others believe that they promote friendship among nations.

Memory Check 2

Match each word and its link to the corresponding definition.

aloof	ambiguous	aggregate
1. a loofa __	2. am big you us __	3. a gray gate __

alleviate	affable	altruistic
4. a leaf he ate __	5. Af a bull __	6. Al True his stick __

anarchist	animosity	ambivalence
7. Anna kissed __	8. Animal City __	9. am Bev Valence __

affirmation	analogous	amorphous
10. a firm mate __	11. Anna Low Gus __	12. am Orphous __

a. open to more than one interpretation
b. active hatred
c. total
d. unselfishly generous
e. apart; reserved
f. comparable
g. relieve
h. assertion; confirmation
i. easily approachable; warmly friendly
j. the state of having contradictory or conflicting emotional attitudes
k. formless; lacking shape or definition
l. a person who seeks to overturn the established government

Showtime 2

Fill in the blanks in the following sentences with the word or set of words that best fits the meaning of the sentence as a whole.

1. As club president, I expect everyone to make an _____ of loyalty.
   a. adulation   b. affirmation   c. aggregate   d. accolade   e. acclaim

2. In economics class, we calculated the _____ wealth of the students in our class.
   a. abstemious   b. abstruse   c. altruistic   d. aesthetic   e. aggregate

3. The wheels of a car are _____ to the legs of a person—both allow movement.
   a. aloof   b. analogous   c. abstract   d. altruistic   e. affable

4. Sue's _____ toward Beth increased after she learned that her boyfriend had been helping Beth with her history homework.

   a. affirmation   b. adulation   c. adversity   d. animosity   e. acclaim

5. My mother is so _____ that she spends most of her spare time _____ the suffering of homeless people in our city.

   a. sympathetic.....acclaiming
   b. altruistic.....alleviating
   c. affable.....acquiescing
   d. abstruse.....acknowledging
   e. aloof.....helping

6. In contrast to Molly, who likes to remain _____ , Sandra, who has a (an) _____ personality, is one of the most popular students in school.

   a. aesthetic.....friendly
   b. apart.....aggressive
   c. alone.....magnetic
   d. abstruse.....interesting
   e. aloof.....affable

7. The speaker's argument was so _____ that it caused only _____ among his audience.

   a. altruistic.....animosity
   b. ambiguous.....adulation
   c. aloof.....adversity
   d. amorphous.....ambivalence
   e. aesthetic.....ambivalence

8. The speech by the _____ was not _____ ; it demanded that all government be completely abolished.

   a. official.....altruistic
   b. adversary.....aloof
   c. leader.....abstract
   d. anarchist.....ambiguous
   e. enemy.....amorphous

anomaly

irregularity

Picture this:
Ann O'Malley

UNIT 3

Ann O'Malley, the only girl who lived in the valley, was an *anomaly*.

■ An *anomaly* in a person's heartbeat should be investigated by a physician.

■ Earth's atmosphere causes *anomalies* in telescopic observation of other planets.

■ Because Fred had always come to work on time, his boss regarded it as an *anomaly* when he arrived an hour late one day.

antagonism (an TAG uh niz um)

actively expressed
hostility

Picture this:
ants tags on

The *antagonism* from the *ants* with
tags on them was unmistakable.

- *Antagonism* developed between the twins, Bill and John,
  after they discovered that each of them had asked the same
  girl to the dance.

- According to psychologists, some *antagonism* between
  siblings is natural as each child seeks parental affection
  and approval.

- Jason knew that he might *antagonize* his history teacher if
  he criticized her teaching methods, but he decided that he
  had no choice because he wasn't learning much in the class.

(an tih duh LOO vee un)

antediluvian

extremely old

Picture this:
Aunty dill luvin'

Aunty Lil, a *dill luvin'* lady, reads tales
of *antediluvian* times.

■ The origins of Egypt are lost in the mists of *antediluvian*
times.

■ Young people today regard black and white TV as an
antediluvian form of technology.

■ "Mom," Tina said to her mother, "your ideas are so
antediluvian. Today, all the girls are getting tattoos."

antidote

(AN tih dote)

medicine to counteract a poison or disease; something that relieves a harmful effect

Picture this:
Aunty dotes

Aunty dotes on her goats that carry *antidotes* to remote places.

■ Researchers are trying to find an *antidote* for the common cold, but so far they have had only limited success.

■ Doctors often say that the best *antidote* for most human ills is time.

■ If you are bitten by a snake, you should try to note its appearance so that the correct *antidote* can be prescribed based on what species of snake bit you.

antiquated

old-fashioned;
obsolete

Picture this:
Aunty equated

Aunty equated Wes with her old flame Jess.
What an *antiquated* mind!

■ Most people regard the phonograph as an example of an *antiquated* technology.

■ Some famous writers prefer to use an *antiquated* typewriter rather than a computer.

■ Although they employed technology that would be considered *antiquated* today, the engineers who designed the Egyptian pyramids were able to cut and move stones that each weighed thousands of tons.

apathy

(AP uh thee)

lack of interest or concern

Picture this:
a path he

By *a path*, *he* sat in *apathy*.

■ Voter *apathy* in the United States is so great that in most elections less than half of the eligible voters turn out to cast their votes.

■ *Apathy* about social and political issues often occurs when people feel that these issues do not directly concern them.

■ After many years of trying without success to become manager, Harry became *apathetic* about striving to get ahead in his career.

(uh PEEZ)	# appease

pacify or soothe;
relieve

Picture this:
o' peas

Tom was *appeasing* a pot *o' peas*.

■ To *appease* liberals in his party who were unhappy with his
conservative policies, the president appointed a liberal to
the Supreme Court.

■ The candy bar that Sharon ate *appeased* her hunger.

■ In order to *appease* the angry voters, Congress voted to
reduce taxes.

apprehension

(ap rih HEN shun)

fearful anticipation
of the future; dread

Picture this:
a pre-hen

This dance is *HUGE.*

A pre-hen, like a pre-teen, feels *apprehension*.

■ Most people think about their own eventual death with *apprehension*.

■ The students facing the test are full of *apprehension* because their future depends on how well they perform on it.

■ Many people are filled with *apprehension* when they have to speak before a large group of people.

(AHR bih trer ee)	arbitrary

Picture this:
our bit's rare

determined by chance or a whim, not by necessity, reason, or principle; based on or subject to individual judgment or preference

"*Our bit's rare*," they complained.
"It's *arbitrary* who gets a rare bit!" shouted the chef.

■ Judges who make *arbitrary* rulings can be removed from office.

■ Mr. Hughes chose students for the class debate in an *arbitrary* manner; he selected every fifth person on the class roster.

■ The decision to use the color green to mean "Go" was an *arbitrary* one.

archaic

(ahr KAY ik)

ancient;
out-of-date

Picture this:
Ark K—Ick!

Sick kangaroos ride on *archaic Ark K—"Ick!"*
is all they can say.

■ The typewriter is regarded by many people today as an *archaic* form of technology.

■ The words *thou* and *thee* are examples of *archaic* English.

■ Students often complain that they have trouble understanding Shakespeare's English because it is *archaic*.

ardent

intense; passionate; zealous

Picture this:
are dents

"*Are dents* on the car?" asks the *ardent* racer.

■ *Ardent* Democrats and Republicans usually vote for the persons nominated by their parties.

■ Even the most *ardent* supporters of freedom of speech believe there must be some limitations on what people are allowed to say.

■ An *ardent* environmentalist, Senator Wood voted for the bill even though it meant a loss of jobs for his state in the mining industry.

arrogance

(AR uh guns)

pride;
haughtiness

Picture this:
Arrow Dance

At the *Arrow Dance*, arrows illustrate *arrogance*.

■ Although he is one of the richest people in America, Sam tries to avoid giving an appearance of *arrogance*; he drives a compact car and eats in fast-food restaurants.

■ People from rich countries visiting poor countries sometimes display *arrogance*, believing themselves to be superior to the local people.

■ Shy people are sometimes accused of *arrogance* because they seem haughty and aloof.

Memory Check 3
Match each word and its link to the corresponding definition.

anomaly   arbitrary   antidote
1. **Ann O'Malley** __   2. **our bit's rare** __   3. **Aunty dotes** __

ardent   antediluvian   antiquated
4. **are dents** __   5. **Aunty dill luvin'** __   6. **Aunty equated** __

apathy   archaic   appease
7. **a path he** __   8. **Ark K—Ick!** __   9. **o' peas** __

antagonism   apprehension   arrogance
10. **ants tags on** __   11. **a pre-hen** __   12. **Arrow Dance** __

a. extremely old
b. dread
c. lack of interest or concern
d. medicine to counteract a poison or disease
e. actively expressed hostility
f. determined by chance or a whim, not by necessity, reason, or principle
g. irregularity
h. old-fashioned; obsolete
i. ancient; out-of-date
j. haughtiness
k. zealous
l. pacify or soothe

Showtime 3
Fill in the blanks in the following sentences with the word or set of words that best fits the meaning of the sentence as a whole.

1. Modern editors of old books frequently change _____ spelling to make them easier to read.
   a. ambiguous b. archaic c. amorphous d. abstract e. interesting

2. No one except the president's most _____ supporters agreed with his new policy.
   a. aloof b. affable c. archaic d. ardent e. altruistic

3. John learned when he was a child that _____ a bully usually just makes the bully demand even more.
   a. alleviating b. knowing c. advocating d. judging e. appeasing

4. The president said that now that victory had been achieved the nation's greatest enemy was _____ .

   a. ardent b. apathy c. archaic d. arbitrary e. apprehension

5. The students in our school regard any teacher over forty years old as _____ ; however, Mr. Young is an _____ because he acts like he's still twenty-five even though he's forty-five.

   a. abstemious.....exception
   b. analogous.....oddity
   c. antediluvian.....anomaly
   d. antiquated.....aggregate
   e. abstruse.....abnormality

6. The _____ against bacterial infections has become _____ as a result of the development of more advanced medicines.

   a. apathy.....amorphous
   b. antagonism.....ambiguous
   c. animosity.....antediluvian
   d. antidote.....antiquated
   e. animosity.....analogous

7. The prisoner awaited the judge's sentence with _____ because the judge was well-known for imposing _____ penalties.

   a. arrogance.....archaic
   b. apprehension.....affable
   c. antagonism.....ardent
   d. adversity.....abstemious
   e. apprehension.....arbitrary

8. The new employee's _____ and "know-it-all" attitude created _____ among the workers.

   a. antagonism.....arrogance
   b. apprehension.....animosity
   c. apathy.....antagonism
   d. arrogance.....antagonism
   e. ambivalence.....affirmation

(ahr TIK yuh lit)	**articulate**

adj: able to express oneself clearly and effectively

Picture this:
R, T, Q lit

UNIT 4

R, T, and *Q lit* the flame. Then *articulate* Q spoke.

■ To become an *articulate* writer, you must write regularly.

■ Improving your vocabulary can help you become more *articulate*.

■ Participating in debates is a good way to become more *articulate* in expressing your ideas.

artifact

object made
by human beings

Picture this:
art a fact

"*Art—a fact* of life in all eras," says Ann
with the *artifact* in her hands.

■ Our history class decided to make a time capsule, so we
gathered various *artifacts* from our everyday life, put them
in a steel box, and buried them in the schoolyard.

■ The pyramids of Egypt are the largest *artifacts* left by
ancient humans.

■ From *artifacts* left by the people of an ancient civilization
scientists can build a picture of how they lived.

artisan

manually skilled worker; craftsperson as opposed to artist

Picture this:
art is sin

"*Art is sin*," says the Puritan to the *artisan*.

■ Potters are *artisans* who can earn a good living by making things that are both useful and attractive.

■ Even in this age of mass production, there is a demand for goods, such as high-quality furniture, that can only be produced by skilled *artisans*.

■ *Artisans* normally earn more money than laborers because they have skills that are in greater demand.

ascendancy

(uh SEN dun see)

controlling influence;
domination

Picture this:
Ascend Dance

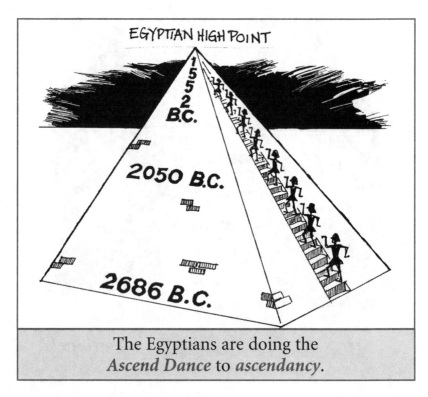

EGYPTIAN HIGH POINT

1552 B.C.

2050 B.C.

2686 B.C.

The Egyptians are doing the
Ascend Dance to *ascendancy*.

■ If one country gains *ascendancy* in a region of the world, its neighbors often band together to try to prevent it from gaining even more power and influence.

■ During the early part of the twentieth century, Nazism was in *ascendancy* in Germany.

■ Over the past decade or so, China has been gaining *ascendancy* among Asian nations.

(uh SET ik)	ascetic

person who leads a life
of self-denial; austere

Picture this:
a set tick

Here sits an *ascetic* listening to *a set tick*.

■ The monk led an *ascetic* life, spending most of his time in prayer and eating only as much as necessary to stay alive.

■ Some religions encourage their followers to practice *asceticism* as a way to purify themselves.

■ Some writers lead an *ascetic* existence when they work on a book, living simply and spending nearly all of their time writing.

aspire

(uh SPY ur)

seek to attain;
long for

Picture this:
a spire

They *aspire* to build *a spire* of straw and
wire for the man with the lyre.

■ Many people *aspire* to be successful novelists, but few
succeed.

■ When he was a high school student, Bill Clinton *aspired*
to be president.

■ Malaysia *aspires* to be a developed country by the
year 2020.

(uh SIJ oo us)	# assiduous

earnest and persistent
in undertaking a task

Picture this:
acid chew us

"Can the *acid chew us*?" "Yes, if we're not
assiduous in keeping the tops on tight!"

■ Bruce is certainly no mathematical genius, but through
assiduous work he managed to get a 620 on the
SAT Math Test.

■ An *assiduous* student in high school, Louis lost a lot of
his interest in studying in college when he made friends
with a group of students whose only interest was partying.

■ Most scientists say that *assiduously* observing and
experimenting is the best way to make a new discovery.

assuage

ease or lessen;
satisfy; soothe

Picture this:
as Sue aged

As Sue aged, only a sage* could *assuage* her rage.

■ After the long and bitter fight for control of the company, the new CEO felt that it was important to *assuage* the angry feelings of all the parties involved.

■ The dying soldier's pain was *assuaged* by the painkiller that the nurse gave him.

■ There's nothing better than cold, pure water to *assuage* your thirst.

* A *sage* is a person venerated for possessing wisdom.

68

(uh STOOT)	astute

wise; shrewd

Picture this:
as toot

To appear *astute*, simply solve
a square root *as* you *toot*.

■ An *astute* editor is able to correct a writer's faulty English without changing the meaning.

■ *Astute* investing by Mrs. Ogden allowed her to buy several vacation homes for her family.

■ Psychologists say that experiments show that females tend to be more *astute* than males at judging the motives of other people.

attribute

(uh TRIB yoot)

explain; relate to a cause

Picture this:
a tribute

BEST
HAIR
OF THE YEAR

His music
is just OK
but his hair
has always
been
GREAT!

They *attribute* his fame to *a tribute* to his mane.

■ America's economic success can be *attributed* to a number of factors, but one of these certainly is the hard work of its people.

■ Small children often *attribute* to their teachers qualities that are almost superhuman.

■ John's reputation for courage was *attributed* to his rescuing a child from a burning building.

(aw DAY shus)	# audacious

daring; bold

Picture this:
all day shush

All day he says "*Shush*" to *audacious*
climbers making a fuss.

■ His plan was an *audacious* one—to climb Mt. Everest solo.

■ President Kennedy set one of the most *audacious* goals of all time when he said that America should land a man on the moon and return him safely to Earth by 1969.

■ Japan's plan at the start of World War II was *audacious*—strike at America quickly before it could build up its military strength.

austere

(aw STEER)

forbiddenly stern; severely
simple and unornamented

Picture this:
Aussie tear

An *Aussie* sheds a *tear*: "It'll be an
austere year without my outback gear."

■ I enjoy the *austere* beauty of the Arizona desert.

■ Monasteries are *austere* places designed to encourage prayer
and reflection.

■ Schoolmasters in colonial America generally were *austere*
figures who inspired fear in their students.

Memory Check 4

Match each word and its link to the corresponding definition.

articulate	ascendancy	artisan
1. R, T, Q lit __	**2. Ascend Dance** __	**3. art is sin** __
austere	assuage	ascetic
4. Aussie tear __	**5. as Sue aged** __	**6. a set tick** __
artifact	audacious	astute
7. art a fact __	**8. all day shush** __	**9. as toot** __
aspire	assiduous	attribute
10. a spire __	**11. acid chew us** __	**12. a tribute** __

a. soothe; satisfy
b. domination
c. person who leads a life of self-denial
d. able to express oneself clearly
e. wise; shrewd
f. craftsperson

g. object made by human beings
h. long for
i. explain; relate to a cause
j. severely simple and unornamented
k. daring; bold
l. persistent in undertaking a task

Showtime 4

Fill in the blanks in the following sentences with the word or set of words that best fits the meaning of the sentence as a whole.

1. Throughout history, the rise of a country to a position of _____ has often led to overconfidence among its people.

   a. arrogance   b. ascendancy   c. adulation
   d. adversity   e. apprehension

2. To _____ his feelings of guilt as a result of his participation in the war, Henry returned to the country in which the war had been fought, after the war ended, to do charity work.

   a. acknowledge   b. assuage   c. advocate   d. attribute   e. acclaim

3. Early humans often _____ magical powers to the forces of nature.

    a. acquiesced   b. articulated   c. advocated   d. attributed   e. aspired

4. The _____ speaker won an award for the best speaker at the debate.

    a. ascetic   b. articulate   c. austere   d. ambiguous   e. abstruse

5. The plan to establish a colony on Mars is an _____ one, but through the _____ efforts of many scientists, engineers, and technicians it might very possibly one day become a reality.

    a. abstruse.....abstemious
    b. astute.....aesthetic
    c. arbitrary.....altruistic
    d. amorphous.....ambiguous
    e. audacious.....assiduous

6. Always an _____ observer of human nature, Karen _____ to become a novelist.

    a. astute.....aspires
    b. affable.....acknowledges
    c. aloof.....admires
    d. assiduous.....assuages
    e. ardent.....acquiesces

7. The _____ lived an _____ life.

    a. adversary.....abstract
    b. anarchist.....audacious
    c. ascetic.....austere
    d. artisan.....aloof
    e. aggregate.....abstemious

8. An _____ made many years ago by Native American _____ was found when workers dug up a road near my house.

    a. antidote.....anarchists
    b. artifact.....artisans
    c. artisan.....artifacts
    d. aggregate.....workers
    e. adversary.....artists

authoritarian

adj: characterized by or favoring strict obedience to authority

noun: a ruler who insists on complete obedience

Picture this:
Arthur Tarian

UNIT 5

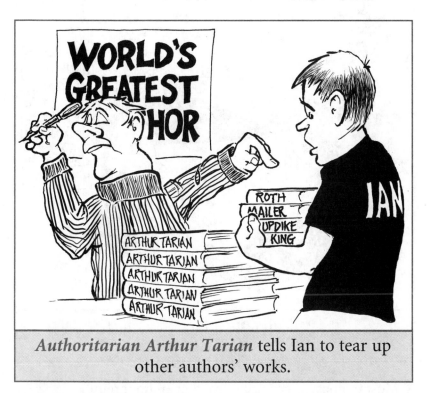

Authoritarian Arthur Tarian tells Ian to tear up other authors' works.

■ *Authoritarian* governments restrict individual rights in order to maintain rigid control over the people.

■ China is becoming less *authoritarian*, allowing individuals more freedom.

■ The *authoritarian* has ruled the country for thirty years.

autonomous

(aw TAH nuh mus)

not controlled by outside
forces; self-governing

Picture this:
aw Tono must

Aw! *Tono must* rely on guano,
but at least it's *autonomous*.

■ Most political scientists believe that an important
characteristic of a democratic country is an *autonomous*
judiciary.

■ In the American system of government, states are not
autonomous; many powers are reserved to the central
government.

■ After the fall of the Soviet Union, many of its former
republics became *autonomous* nation-states.

avarice

greediness for wealth

Picture this:
have a rice

"*Have a rice* cracker; you're in luck—it's only
ten bucks!" (What *avarice*!)

■ According to psychologists, many gamblers are motivated
not by *avarice* but by a need for excitement.

■ It was not *avarice* that motivated Joe to work hard to
become wealthy so much as a desire for financial security.

■ Although Lou was not really an *avaricious* person, he did
find the idea of winning the twenty million dollar lottery
prize attractive.

aversion

(uh VUR zhen)

firm dislike

Picture this:
a version

He has an *aversion* to *a version* of baked sturgeon
cooked by his wife, a plastic surgeon.

■ I have an *aversion* to spicy food because it upsets my
stomach.

■ Sue has such an *aversion* to cigarette smoke that she can't
stand being in a room in which even one person is smoking.

■ An *aversion* to spiders is found in people all over the world.

beguile

charm; mislead
or delude

Picture this:
be Guy ill

Be Guy well, or *be Guy ill*,
he must *beguile* the nurse from Brazil.

■ The con man *beguiled* my mother with a sob story about how his child needed money for an operation.

■ Many British soldiers enlisted in the army in World War I because they were *beguiled* by the idea of taking part in a quick and glorious victory.

■ A good magician uses a number of tricks to *beguile* his audience into believing that what they're seeing is real.

belie

(bih LYE)

contradict; give
a false impression

Picture this:
bee lie

The *bee* tells a *lie* that *belies* its nasty sting.

- The small size of the Australian funnel web spider *belies* the deadliness of its venom.

- His kind words were *belied* by his angry tone and expression.

- Ms. Johnson's small size *belies* the ferocity with which she can scold a student who doesn't hand in an assignment on time.

benevolent

generous;
charitable

Picture this:
Ben never lent

Ben was a true gem.
. . . one of the most
benevolent men
that ever lived.

*"Benevolent? Ben never
lent anything to anyone."*

■ Children in America imagine Santa Claus as a *benevolent* old man who dispenses gifts on Christmas.

■ America relies on private *benevolent* foundations to help many people faced with financial difficulties.

■ "Mr. Zimmerman must have been in a *benevolent* mood when he marked our history tests," Joan said. "This is the first time nobody failed."

benign

(bih NINE)

showing gentleness;
exerting a beneficial
influence; harmless

Picture this:
Bee 9

Bee 9 buzzes by *benign* roses in *benign* weather.

■ The king's *benign* rule has made him popular with his subjects.

■ The senator supports the new policy because she believes it will have *benign* consequences for the economy.

■ According to the computer expert, a trojan horse is a malicious program that passes itself off as a *benign* application.

bolster

support;
reinforce

Picture this:
bowl stir

In the *bowl stir* the batter
to *bolster* the boys' morale!

■ Knowing a lot of difficult words will *bolster* your
confidence when you take the SAT.

■ A good manager knows when to criticize an employee
and when to *bolster* his or her confidence with praise.

■ Britain and its allies were *bolstered* by the entry of the
United States into World War II in 1941.

bombastic

(bom BAS tik)

pompous; using
inflated language

Picture this:
bomb's tick

The *bombastic* speaker doesn't hear
the *bomb's tick*.

■ Today, *bombastic* speeches are criticized for their pomposity, but in the past many people enjoyed them as entertainment.

■ A *bombastic* piece of writing may impress some readers, but others will surely conclude that its author is an insincere and pretentious person.

■ Be careful of putting all the SAT-type words you've learned into your essays; you might think they sound impressive, but your teacher will probably say that your writing is *bombastic*.

(BRAG ert)	braggart

boaster

Picture this:
Brag Art

The *Brag Art* Exhibition of *braggart* art.

■ Mandy's mom turned into a bit of a *braggart* after her daughter made the all-state soccer team.

■ *Braggarts* are annoying—especially when their boasts turn out to be correct!

■ Our basketball team has a *braggart* who says that no one can outshoot her from either the field or the free throw line.

cajole

coax

Picture this:
Cajun Joel

Cajun Joel cajoles the frog into a roll
and eats it whole.

- Most children are pretty good at *cajoling* their parents into buying them toys.

- Joe Sellers considered himself one of the company's top salespeople; he bragged that he could *cajole* an Alaskan into buying an air conditioner in the winter.

- We *cajoled* Dad into taking us to the Major League Baseball All-Star Game this year.

Memory Check 5

Match each word and its link to the corresponding definition.

avarice	authoritarian	braggart
1. **have a rice** __	2. **Arthur Tarian** __	3. **Brag Art** __
benevolent	beguile	bolster
4. **Ben never lent** __	5. **be Guy ill** __	6. **bowl stir** __
benign	aversion	autonomous
7. **Bee 9** __	8. **a version** __	9. **aw Tono must** __
belie	bombastic	cajole
10. **bee lie** __	11. **bomb's tick** __	12. **Cajun Joel** __

a. greediness for wealth
b. give a false impression
c. self-governing
d. using inflated language
e. generous
f. firm dislike

g. charm; mislead or delude
h. a ruler who insists on complete obedience
i. coax
j. harmless
k. support
l. boaster

Showtime 5

Fill in the blanks in the following sentences with the word or set of words that best fits the meaning of the sentence as a whole.

1. Jane was so _____ by the "easy" monthly payment plan offered by the car salesperson that she spent more money than she could afford on her car.

   a. belied   b. appeased   c. assuaged   d. beguiled   e. bolstered

2. Our school's top lineman Jim "Jumbo" Jones' 300-pound frame _____ his impressive speed over forty yards.

   a. cajoles   b. acknowledges   c. belies   d. acclaims   e. attributes

3. The businessman was known for his _____ ; he cared about nothing except increasing his profits so he could become wealthy.

   a. aversion   b. arrogance   c. apathy   d. avarice   e. ambivalence

4. The wealthy industrialist underwent a great change after seeing the suffering of people in Africa and became _____ ; he donated half of his fortune to charities there.

    a. affable   b. abstemious   c. autonomous   d. benevolent   e. bombastic

5. John hates going to the doctor, but his wife _____ him to go to have a mole that had changed color tested; thankfully, the test showed that it was _____.

    a. belied.....antiquated
    b. beguiled.....benovolent
    c. acclaimed.....antiquated
    d. acknowledged.....bombastic
    e. cajoled.....benign

6. _____ often boast of their abilities in order to _____ their self-confidence.

    a. Authoritarians.....alleviate
    b. Braggarts.....bolster
    c. Aggregates.....acknowledge
    d. Anarchists.....appease
    e. Ascetics.....belie

7. The _____ government rejected the newspaper's request to allow it to be more _____ in reporting the news.

    a. autonomous.....audacious
    b. astute.....aloof
    c. authoritarian.....autonomous
    d. antiquated.....altruistic
    e. audacious.....arbitrary

8. Most English teachers have an _____ to the _____ language sometimes used by students to make their writing seem impressive.

    a. antidote.....abstemious
    b. antagonism.....astute
    c. adulation.....ambiguous
    d. aversion.....bombastic
    e. arrogance.....abstract

(KAL kyuh lay tid)	**calculated**

deliberately
planned

Picture this:
calculate Ted

UNIT 6

"I *calculate Ted* is late for calculus for no *calculated* reason. Just California dreamin'."

■ Baseball managers sometimes take *calculated* risks, such as calling for a double steal.

■ The comedian's performance appeared unrehearsed; however, we found out later that every line was carefully *calculated* to get a laugh from the audience.

■ I was disappointed to find out that Bill's every move was *calculated* to win our boss's favor and make me look bad.

candor

(KAN der)

frankness;
open honesty

Picture this:
can door

"A *can* with a *door*? Honestly, *I* didn't do it!"
he says with *candor*.

■ It's unrealistic to expect people to speak with *candor* at all times.

■ It seems to be human nature to expect *candor* from others when we speak to them but not to also expect it from ourselves.

■ Talk show hosts are good at getting guests to speak *candidly* about their lives.

capricious

unpredictable;
fickle

Picture this:
Capri

We can never predict what they'll be doing at three o'clock.

Off the isle of *Capri*, *capricious* dolphins
play at three.

■ "The weather has been *capricious* recently," Bill said, "so,
I think I'll skip the picnic I planned with my friends and
just order a pizza."

■ My cat is a *capricious* eater; every day she wants something
different to eat.

■ Science operates on the assumption that the laws of nature
are not *capricious*.

censure

(SEN sher)

express formal disapproval; blame; criticize

Picture this:
cent sore

A *cent* with a *sore censured* at the Century Bank.

- The judge was *censured* for injudicious conduct.

- Professional bodies have the power to *censure* members who violate their code of ethics.

- The State Department *censures* countries that allow the human rights of their citizens to be violated.

charlatan

a quack; pretender

Picture this:
Charlotte Tan

Charlotte Tan with a *charlatan*.

■ Jack pretended to be a linguist with a vast knowledge of foreign languages; however, he was exposed as a *charlatan* when he couldn't even tell us the meaning of *au revoir*.

■ The history of medicine is filled with *charlatans* who promised cures for incurable illnesses.

■ A *charlatan* sold me a watch worth $5 for $50.

coalesce

(koh uh LES)

combine;
fuse

Picture this:
coal-less

The "*coal-less*" people of Coalsville
coalesce around the coal strike issue.

■ To work together successfully, military units must *coalesce*
to become a group of like-minded individuals.

■ The United States began to *coalesce* as a nation during the
early nineteenth century as the experiences of many groups
were communicated around the country.

■ Our business plan began to *coalesce* in our minds after
several discussions.

(kuh LOW kwee ul)	colloquial

pertaining to conversational or common speech

Picture this:
call oak we all

When we hear the *call* to gather near the *oak*, *we all* speak in *colloquial* terms.

■ *Colloquial* speech helps the members of a group of people identify themselves as different from others.

■ *Colloquial* words and expressions should not be used in formal English.

■ "OK" is an American *colloquial* expression that is used around the world.

compile

assemble; gather;
accumulate

Picture this:
come pile

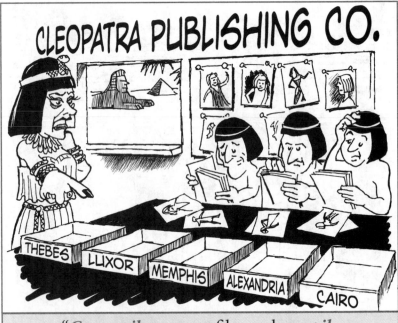

"*Come, pile* up your files and *compile*
The Styles of the Nile!*"

■ Newspapers *compile* information from many sources in order to give readers a wide view of what is happening in the world.

■ After every season, the batting average and other statistics for every player in Major League Baseball are *compiled*.

■ A good prosecutor *compiles* evidence steadily until a convincing case is made of the defendant's guilt.

complacency

self-satisfaction;
smugness

Picture this:
come place cents he

"*Come*, *place cents* on Clancy. *He* is
sure to win," he says with *complacency*.

■ *Complacency* among employees is a problem sometimes
faced by managers of successful companies.

■ Some experts believe that Japanese industry became
complacent after its great success in the 1980s.

■ Health workers urged parents to guard against *complacency*
and make sure that their children are immunized against
measles and other infectious diseases.

compliance

(kum PLY uns)

readiness to yield;
conformity

Picture this:
come ply ants

"*Come, ply ants* with honey to gain their
compliance with our plan."

■ Unless you'd like to spend some time in jail, *compliance*
with the regulations of the Internal Revenue Service is
advisable.

■ General Rogers did not expect every soldier to support his
every command enthusiastically; however, he did expect
their *compliance*.

■ The president called Senator Balky to try to get her
compliance on the crucial vote.

composure

mental
calmness

Picture this:
calm pose sure

"With only a rose, can I keep a *calm pose*?
Sure, I can keep my *composure*!"

■ While executing a double axel, the figure skater fell and
became upset for a while; however, he soon regained his
composure and completed his routine successfully.

■ A platoon leader must have *composure* under enemy fire
so he can make the correct decisions.

■ With two minutes to go on a section of the SAT, John
realized he had filled in the ovals out of order; he kept his
composure, however, and corrected his mistake before the
time was up.

comprehensive   *(kom prih HEN siv)*

thorough;
all-inclusive

Picture this:
come pre-hens if

"*Come*, *pre-hens*, *if* you can. Join our
comprehensive study of pre-hen behavior."

■ The new U.S. president ordered a *comprehensive* review
of the armed forces.

■ A good dictionary must have a *comprehensive* list of the
words used in a language.

■ Every ten years, a *comprehensive* census is conducted by
the U.S. government.

Memory Check 6

Match each word and its link to the corresponding definition.

calculated
1. **calculate Ted** __

complacency
2. **come place**
   cents he __

censure
3. **cent sore** __

comprehensive
4. **come pre-hens if** __

charlatan
5. **Charlotte Tan** __

composure
6. **calm pose sure** __

compile
7. **come pile** __

candor
8. **can door** __

colloquial
9. **call oak we all** __

capricious
10. **Capri** __

coalesce
11. **coal-less** __

compliance
12. **come ply ants** __

a. blame
b. deliberately planned
c. readiness to yield
d. unpredictable
e. gather; accumulate
f. pretender

g. combine
h. mental calmness
i. pertaining to common speech
j. self-satisfaction
k. frankness
l. thorough

Showtime 6

Fill in the blanks in the following sentences with the word or set of words that best fits the meaning of the sentence as a whole.

1. Don't make a (an) _____ decision when choosing a college to attend; you might regret it.

   a. calculated   b. astute   c. capricious   d. benevolent   e. ardent

2. When visiting another country _____ with its customs is advisable.

   a. complacency   b. apathy   c. antagonism
   d. animosity   e. compliance

3. Although Jim had been wrongly charged with the murder, he kept his _____ and calmly explained that he had been in New York on the day that the crime was committed in Dallas.

   a. candor   b. compliance   c. composure
   d. complacency   e. ascendancy

4. The difference in opinion between the two sides on this issue is so great that a (an) _____ solution seems highly unlikely.

   a. comprehensive   b. bombastic   c. amorphous
   d. colloquial   e. capricious

5. We decided to sue the _____ because he had made a (an) _____ and systematic effort to deceive our company into believing he was a qualified lawyer.

   a. braggart.....bombastic
   b. charlatan.....calculated
   c. adversary.....capricious
   d. anarchist.....amorphous
   e. ascetic.....altruistic

6. The English teacher asked the class to _____ a list of _____ expressions used by teenagers today.

   a. compile.....colloquial
   b. coalesce.....comprehensive
   c. acknowledge.....colloquial
   d. censure.....capricious
   e. collect.....comprehensive

7. After the public's initial _____ about the growing problem, support began to _____ around a plan to take action to solve it.

   a. apprehension.....bolster
   b. compliance.....acquiesce
   c. candor.....compile
   d. ambivalence.....articulate
   e. complacency.....coalesce

8. The government official was _____ for lack of _____ in his testimony before Congress.

   a. compiled.....compliance
   b. censured.....honesty
   c. acclaimed.....candor
   d. acknowledged.....compliance
   e. advocated.....adversity

concede

admit;
yield

Picture this:
cons' seed

UNIT 7

"I *concede* that it's the *cons' seed*, but I need feed!"

■ Our tennis team *conceded* the match after it was discovered that one of our players had not been academically eligible to play.

■ I *concede* that I don't know much about the history of music.

■ Jim *conceded* that Bob had made some good points during the debate but refused to admit that Bob had made a better overall argument.

conciliatory

overcoming hostility
or distrust

Picture this:
con's silly story

The *con's silly story*—a *conciliatory* gesture.

■ After her argument with her boyfriend, Jane made a *conciliatory* gesture and bought him a book by his favorite author.

■ The "good cop, bad cop" routine allows one person to be harsh and rigid with another party while the other person is *conciliatory*.

■ After Senator Smith won the bitterly fought election for governor, she decided to be *conciliatory* toward her defeated opponent and offered him a job in her cabinet.

(kun SICE)	concise

brief and
compact

Picture this:
cons' ice

A message *concise—cons' ice*.

■ Judge Jones is famous for demanding a *concise* summary of the events in cases that she hears.

■ Lincoln's "Gettysburg Address" is a model of *concise* writing.

■ "Will you marry me?" asked Walter. "Yes" was Sally's *concise* answer.

conflagration　*(kon fluh GRAY shun)*

great fire

Picture this:
con flag ration

A *con flag ration* after the
prison flag *conflagration*.

- During World War II, Allied bombing of Tokyo caused a *conflagration* in that city.

- The retreating army started a *conflagration* in order to destroy supplies that could be used by the advancing forces.

- Firefighters in large cities with many high-rise buildings must be careful not to allow a small fire to spread quickly and become a *conflagration*.

(kun FOUND)	confound

confound;
puzzle

Picture this:
con found

What the *con found confounds* him.

■ Until Louis Pasteur discovered germs, the origin of many diseases *confounded* scientists.

■ The American watching a cricket match in Britain was *confounded* by the complex rules of the game.

■ Many statements that students make in their essays are *confounding* to teachers when they are poorly written.

contend
(kun TEND)

assert
earnestly

Picture this:
con tends

He *contends* that a *con tends* to return.

■ In our next debate, our team must *contend* that "Science has done more harm than good."

■ A good lawyer must be able to *contend* convincingly that her client is innocent even if she feels sure that he is guilty.

■ People known as "flat-earthers" *contend* that Earth is flat rather than round as most people believe.

contentious

quarrelsome;
causing quarrels

Picture this:
content shush

"The kids are *content*. *Shush*!
Don't be so *contentious*!"

■ I suggest that we avoid discussing *contentious* subjects such as religion and politics until we get to know one another better.

■ To help unify the party after the hard-fought election campaign, the president asked that *contentious* issues not be discussed for three months.

■ Jean seems to be a naturally *contentious* person; I said the weather seems fine today and she replied that it wasn't true because there were some clouds in the sky.

conviction

strongly held belief;
judgment that someone
is guilty of a crime

Picture this:
convict shun

"It is my *conviction* that every
convict should *shun* crime."

■ During a debate, you should speak with *conviction* to help persuade the judges of the correctness of your argument.

■ For a democracy to remain strong and healthy, people must voice their *convictions* freely.

■ The prosecutor celebrated after winning the first *conviction* of his career.

(KOR jil)

cordial

gracious;
heartfelt

Picture this:
cord Jill

"I've cut the *cord*, *Jill!*"
(Relations are no longer *cordial*.)

■ Despite being separated, Bill and Laura still have *cordial* relations with one another.

■ The principal gave the new teachers a *cordial* welcome at the teacher orientation.

■ Diplomats work hard to maintain *cordial* relations with their colleagues from other countries so that disputes can be discussed in a friendly atmosphere.

corrode

(kuh ROAD)

destroy by chemical
action; deteriorate

Picture this:
car rode

In the old *car* she *rode* until it *corroded*.

■ Water pipes in many cities built early in the last century are beginning to *corrode*.

■ People who live near the ocean often complain that the salty air *corrodes* parts of their houses, such as metal window fixtures.

■ If the chassis of your car starts to *corrode*, you should have it repaired before it becomes worse.

(kry TEER ee un)	criterion

standard used
in judging

Picture this:
cry tear on

"You didn't meet the *criterion* for the team?
Come, *cry* a *tear on* my shoulder."

■ One *criterion* for a good vocabulary-building book is that
words are reinforced in the student's mind.

■ Many universities include the ability to write clear and
correct English as one of their admissions *criteria*.

■ Studies show that the most important *criterion* students
use in judging the effectiveness of a teacher is his or her
knowledge of the subject.

cryptic

(KRIP tik)

mysterious;
hidden; secret

Picture this:
crypt tick

A *cryptic crypt tick*.

■ The only reply Mrs. Thomas got from her daughter Jessica when she asked her where she had been was a *cryptic* "Out."

■ Sharon got her essay back and was surprised to see that her teacher had written only a *cryptic* comment: "Hmm."

■ The historian believed that he had found a *cryptic* message buried in the old text.

Memory Check 7

Match each word and its link to the corresponding definition.

corrode	confound	contentious
1. **car rode** __	2. **con found** __	3. **content shush** __
concise	contend	conviction
4. **cons' ice** __	5. **con tends** __	6. **convict shun** __
conciliatory	cordial	concede
7. **con's silly story** __	8. **cord Jill** __	9. **cons' seed** __
conflagration	criterion	cryptic
10. **con flag ration** __	11. **cry tear on** __	12. **crypt tick** __

a. assert earnestly
b. gracious; heartfelt
c. deteriorate
d. strongly held belief
e. brief and compact
f. standard used in judging

g. quarrelsome; causing quarrels
h. confuse; puzzle
i. overcoming hostility
j. great fire
k. admit
l. hidden; secret

Showtime 7

Fill in the blanks in the following sentences with the word or set of words that best fits the meaning of the sentence as a whole.

1. When you write a resume to apply for a job, you should make it _____ so that your prospective employer can get a quick idea of your background.
   a. comprehensive   b. cordial   c. cryptic   d. contentious   e. concise

2. The designers of the SAT _____ that the test is a fair measure of a student's academic ability.
   a. confound   b. cajole   c. concede   d. contend   e. compile

3. Despite the _____ , the fireman rescued the family from their burning home.
   a. conflagration   b. candor   c. complacency
   d. conviction   e. charlatan

4. The caller left only a _____ message on my answering machine— "I'm finished."

    a. conciliatory   b. colloquial   c. cordial   d. comprehensive   e. cryptic

5. After his many years of staunch opposition to the proposal, Mr. Willis _____ the voters when, in a (an) _____ move, he agreed to seriously reconsider it.

    a. appeased.....ambiguous
    b. beguiled.....affable
    c. confounded.....conciliatory
    d. acknowledged.....contentious
    e. censured.....benevolent

6. An important _____ that airlines must use in hiring a person as part of their cabin crew is that he or she must be _____ .

    a. conviction.....affable
    b. affirmation.....assiduous
    c. accolade.....benevolent
    d. criterion.....cordial
    e. artifact.....conciliatory

7. After their many bitter disputes about the _____ issue dividing their nations, trust between the two leaders began to _____ .

    a. conciliatory.....compile
    b. contentious.....corrode
    c. concise.....concede
    d. ambiguous.....confound
    e. comprehensive.....contend

8. Although Peter has a (an) _____ that people should have freedom of speech, he _____ that there must at times be limitations placed on that freedom.

    a. aversion.....contends
    b. affirmation.....acknowledges
    c. conviction.....concedes
    d. belief.....contentious
    e. doubt.....advocates

culpable

deserving
blame

Picture this:
cool pebble

UNIT 8

Sue's *cool pebble* is missing,
and Beth is *culpable*.

■ The police investigation narrowed down the list of suspects to three people, one of whom was considered most likely to be *culpable*.

■ Suspects cannot be held unless there is reasonable evidence that they are *culpable*.

■ The principal found Jim *culpable* of cheating on the exam and suspended him from school for a week.

cursory

done with haste and little attention to detail

Picture this:
curse sorry

"Did I *curse*? *Sorry*!"—a *cursory* apology.

■ Many pilots make a final *cursory* inspection of their aircraft shortly before takeoff.

■ A *cursory* analysis of the problem revealed a possible cause; however, a more thorough analysis would be needed to determine whether or not the actual cause had been identified.

■ An experienced editor can tell from a *cursory* reading of a manuscript whether or not the writer is using correct English.

debilitate

(dih BILL ih tayt)

weaken;
enfeeble

Picture this:
da bill it ate

Da bill it ate debilitates the billy goat.

■ During very hot weather, it's important to drink plenty of water so as not to become *debilitated* as a result of dehydration.

■ Diseases *debilitate* many people in Africa who don't have adequate nutrition and lack access to modern medicine.

■ Injuries sustained in automobile accidents *debilitate* thousands of people in the United States each year.

decorum

(dih KOR um)

orderliness and good
taste in manners

Picture this:
décor* room

"Such refined *décor*. The *room* is lovely."
(A show of *decorum* as she enters the room.)

- The senior prom gave the usually rowdy Jack a chance to show us that he could behave with *decorum*.

- Expecting *decorum* in a kindergarten class is unrealistic.

- Students in the junior high cafeteria behaved with *decorum* until a food fight that soon involved every student broke out.

* *Décor* refers to the style of decoration of a room.

degradation

(deg ruh DAY shun)

humiliation;
degeneration

Picture this:
"D" grade date shun

What a date!
How humiliating.

I'd give it a "D"
for sure.

Yeah, "D" for Dire!

BORN TO BOOGIE

Degradation from a *"D" grade date—shun* it!

■ The deliberate *degradation* of prisoners of war is prohibited under the Geneva Convention.

■ After many years of military service and disrepair, the navy vessel's effectiveness in combat was significantly *degraded*.

■ The satellite was placed in such a low Earth orbit that the orbit *degraded* after only two days, and the satellite fell to Earth.

deplore

(dih PLOR)

regret;
disapprove of

Picture this:
deep lore*

"I *deplore deep lore*," says the shallow bore.

- Many people *deplore* the showing of extreme violence on television.

- The president said that he *deplored* the loss of life in the battle but granted that such losses were unavoidable.

- My grandfather *deplores* the increasing commercialization of major sports such as football and baseball.

* *Lore* refers to the legends or beliefs of a group of people.

depravity

extreme corruption;
wickedness

Picture this:
deep rabbit he

Deep in the *rabbit* warren, *he* tells them
a tale of *depravity*.

■ War often brings out the most extreme forms of *depravity*
in human beings, such as the use of torture.

■ Many people believe that without civilization humanity
would sink into *depravity*.

■ The citizens' committee on censorship decided that no
form of *depravity* should be portrayed in the newspaper.

deprecate

(DEP rih kayt)

express disapproval
of; belittle

Picture this:
Dep-Wreck 8

Near *Dep-Wreck 8*, they *deprecate*
the "Catch of the Day."

■ Linda enjoyed her creative writing class because her teacher
never *deprecated* the stories she wrote, but instead always
praised what was good about them.

■ Bob Dylan's singing was *deprecated* by many people;
nevertheless, he became one of the most famous singers
in the history of popular music.

■ After the principal *deprecated* the new teacher in front
of her class, the students lost their respect for her.

124

(dih RIDE)	deride

ridicule;
make fun of

Picture this:
Deer Ride

The **Deer Ride** is awesome, but the other rides are totally lame.

Yeah, **Bird** and **Bear** rides are bogus!

DEER RIDE

BIRD RIDE

BEAR RIDE

They *deride* all rides except for the *Deer Ride*.

- Attempts to use radio waves for long-range communication were *derided* by early twentieth-century physicists as impossible.

- Every time Larry tried to diet, his friends *derided* his effort to lose weight as futile.

- Some people *deride* the study of art as a waste of time.

derivative

unoriginal; derived
from another source

Picture this:
dear river

"*Dear river*, from you all creeks are *derivative*!"

■ Few works of art are truly original; nearly all are *derivative* in that they use the ideas and styles of earlier works.

■ American Impressionism is a *derivative* style; American artists adapted European Impressionism to create a new style.

■ Critics agree that the new novel is merely *derivative*, offering nothing new in either style or content.

deterrent

something that
discourages

Picture this:
debt her rent

Never mind, you can have free rent until you get back on your feet.

As a *deterrent* to *debt, her rent*
is waived for a while.

■ The library's policy of allowing students to take out only
one book at a time is a *deterrent* to reading.

■ The government imposes a high tax on cigarettes as a
deterrent to smoking.

■ The United States maintains a powerful military force
as a *deterrent* to aggression by other countries.

digress

wander away
from the subject

Picture this:
tigress

The *tigress* likes to *digress*.

- Some students in history class think Mr. Romano *digresses* too much, but I don't agree because I learn interesting facts that aren't in the textbook.

- If you *digress* when you write an essay, your writing will lack focus and contain irrelevant information.

- The judge instructed the witness to stop *digressing* and stick to the main events in her account of the incident.

Memory Check 8

Match each word and its link to the corresponding definition.

deprecate
1. **Dep-Wreck 8** __

culpable
2. **cool pebble** __

debilitate
3. **da bill it ate** __

deplore
4. **deep lore** __

degradation
5. **"D" grade date shun** __

deride
6. **Deer Ride** __

decorum
7. **decor room** __

derivative
8. **dear river** __

digress
9. **tigress** __

cursory
10. **curse sorry** __

depravity
11. **deep rabbit he** __

deterrent
12. **debt her rent** __

a. regret; disapprove of
b. humiliation; degeneration
c. wickedness
d. weaken
e. deserving blame
f. make fun of

g. hastily done
h. good taste in manners
i. unoriginal
j. belittle
k. something that discourages
l. wander away from the subject

Showtime 8

Fill in the blanks in the following sentences with the word or set of words that best fits the meaning of the sentence as a whole.

1. Every member of the aircrew felt _____ after the 18-hour flight from New York to Tokyo.

   a. amorphous   b. debilitated   c. deprecated   d. derivative   e. derided

2. Even a _____ inspection of my tools showed that they had rusted as a result of being left in the rain for a week.

   a. culpable   b. cursory   c. calculated   d. comprehensive   e. derivative

3. Nearly all people agree that the worst forms of _____ should be illegal.

   a. complacency   b. digression   c. arrogance   d. depravity   e. decorum

4. Dr. Johnson, my writing instructor, says that my work is too _____ and that I should try to be more original.

    a. derivative b. cursory c. contentious d. concise e. cryptic

5. Slavery results in the _____ of human beings and in modern times has been _____ and banned by every country in the world.

    a. compliance.....censured
    b. antagonism.....articulated
    c. decorum.....conceded
    d. animosity.....advocated
    e. degradation.....deplored

6. The teacher said that every student in the class would be considered _____ if anyone failed to act with _____ when the officials from the Department of Education visited.

    a. guilty.....animosity
    b. accountable.....antagonism
    c. culpable.....decorum
    d. autonomous.....compliance
    e. contentious.....composure

7. My history teacher _____ my research paper because its lengthy _____ made it difficult for her to follow its main argument.

    a. derided.....conflagrations
    b. deprecated.....digressions
    c. corroded.....artifacts
    d. deplored.....ascetics
    e. debilitated.....digressions

8. The use of nuclear missiles as a _____ against aggression by other countries is _____ by many people as a policy that will lead to the destruction of the entire human race.

    a. deterrent.....derided
    b. derivative.....deplored
    c. digression.....conceded
    d. compliance.....deprecated
    e. decorum.....derided

(DIL uh juns)	diligence

steadiness of effort;
persistent hard work

Picture this:
dill gents

UNIT 9

Remember, every pickle in a jar of Dill Gents must be perfectly pickled.

Dill gents are pickled with *diligence*.

■ Learning a foreign language requires *diligence* on the part of a student.

■ *Diligence* is only one of the requirements for success; another is the application of intelligence.

■ Work *diligently* in all your subjects so that you can reach your full potential.

disclose (dih SKLOZ)

reveal

Picture this:
disc close

"How does the *disc close*? I cannot *disclose* that information."

■ For tax purposes, the government requires that anyone earning an income *disclose* its source.

■ A journalist can sometimes obtain information from a person if the journalist agrees not to *disclose* the source of that information.

■ Aunt Becky has never *disclosed* the name of the man she was going to be married to thirty years ago but who died in a car crash just before the wedding.

(dis KOUNT)	discount

disregard;
dismiss

Picture this:
disc count

He must *discount* the throw in the *disc count*.

■ Until someone saw him having dinner with a woman in a restaurant, the students *discounted* the rumor that the school's oldest bachelor, Mr. Leonard, was going to be married.

■ The report *discounted* the story he was told because it contradicted all the other information he had about the situation.

■ People who work for intelligence services such as the CIA must learn what information they should *discount* and which they should analyze carefully.

discriminating (dih SKRIM uh nay ting)

able to see
differences

Picture this:
disc criminal

A *disc criminal* with *discriminating* taste.

■ A *discriminating* reader, Ms. Hansen chooses books that
have been highly praised by respected reviewers.

■ Lucy's parents want her to become more *discriminating* in
her choice of boyfriends.

■ Gail has *discriminating* taste in chocolate; she can tell with
one bite if a piece of chocolate is high quality.

disdain

scorn

Picture this:
dis Dane

Dis Dane scorns all other dogs.

Dis Dane has *disdain* for the Collie,
the Pug, and the Dalmatian.

■ The soldier was treated with *disdain* by his comrades because he fled the battle after the first shot was fired.

■ Dishonest individuals are regarded with *disdain* by most people.

■ In summarizing what the convicted man had done, the judge made no attempt to hide her *disdain* for a person who would abandon his own children.

disinclination *(dis in kluh NAY shun)*

a reluctance or a lack of enthusiasm

Picture this:
dis incline nation

In *dis incline nation*, folks have
a *disinclination* to walk uphill.

■ Mr. Tanner's son Ike told his father that he had a *disinclination* to spend a beautiful Saturday afternoon mowing the lawn. His father's reply was "That's fine, as long as you understand that I will then have a *disinclination* to pay your allowance this week."

■ Arthur, a slightly built young man, has a *disinclination* to participate in sports involving physical contact.

■ I have a *disinclination* to help you because you didn't help me when I was having difficulties.

dismiss

put away from
consideration; reject

Picture this:
dis miss

I assume your
chocolates are Swiss.
I won't tolerate
any other kind.

Dis, Miss,
is all Swiss.
We don't
serve any
other kind.

Dis Miss will *dismiss* chocolates
that aren't Swiss.

■ My boss asked me for suggestions to improve efficiency but then *dismissed* my ideas as ridiculous.

■ Before you *dismiss* a new idea as impractical, consider it carefully.

■ The company director *dismissed* reports that he was planning to resign, saying there was no basis for such speculation.

disperse

scatter

Picture this:
dis purse

Dis purse is full of really cool stuff!

The contents of *dis purse* are *dispersed*.

■ Tear gas was used to *disperse* the large crowd of angry protesters that had gathered outside the government offices.

■ Biologists believe that every organism is born with the urge to *disperse* its genes as widely as possible.

■ At the sound of the bell signaling the end of the final period of the final day of the school year, the students of Thomas Jefferson High School *dispersed* almost instantaneously.

argumentative;
fond of arguing

Picture this:
dispute 8 just

Dispute 8. Just another dispute
between *disputatious* dates.

■ Mary seems naturally *disputatious*; she takes an extreme position on every issue.

■ Phil has hardly a *disputatious* bone in his body; he'll agree with practically everything you say.

■ The *disputatious* customer disagreed with everything that she was told by the manager.

dissent

disagree

Picture this:
dis scent

Dis scent makes him *dissent*.

- No one *dissented*, so the motion was passed unanimously.

- Courage is often required for a person to *dissent* from the opinion of the majority.

- Justice Smith wrote the *dissenting* opinion for the minority.

divergent

varying; going in
different directions
from the same point

Picture this:
Di verge gent

Di on the *verge* of going with
a *gent* on a *divergent* path.

■ Sandra and Peter took *divergent* approaches to solving the
equation, but both arrived at the correct answer.

■ Paul and Sylvester were good friends in high school, but
their lives took *divergent* paths after high school: Paul
enlisted in the Navy and sails around the world, while
Sylvester has settled down in our hometown.

■ It's often more interesting to listen to a discussion between
experts with *divergent* views than to a discussion in which
similar views are expressed.

document

verb: provide written, photographic, or other forms of evidence

noun: something, such as a photograph or a recording, that can be used to furnish evidence

Picture this:
Doc U meant

Doc U meant to *document* the case.

- The job of a biographer is made easier if the subject has *documented* his or her life.

- Dad likes to *document* our summer vacation trips by recording highlights with his video camera.

- The judge accepted the *documents* provided by the witness as evidence.

Memory Check 9

Match each word and its link to the corresponding definition.

diligence	disclose	disdain
1. **dill gents** __	2. **disc close** __	3. **dis Dane** __
disputatious	divergent	document
4. **dispute 8 just** __	5. **Di verge gent** __	6. **Doc U meant** __
discount	disinclination	disperse
7. **disc count** __	8. **dis incline nation** __	9. **dis purse** __
dismiss	discriminating	dissent
10. **dis Miss** __	11. **disc criminal** __	12. **dis scent** __

a. able to see differences
b. scatter
c. persistent hard work
d. disagree
e. provide written, photographic, or other forms of evidence
f. scorn
g. reveal
h. a reluctance or a lack of enthusiasm
i. put away from consideration
j. varying
k. argumentative
l. disregard; dismiss

Showtime 9

Fill in the blanks in the following sentences with the word or set of words that best fits the meaning of the sentence as a whole.

1. Jim's girlfriend would like him to become more _____ in his taste in clothes.

   a. discriminating   b. arbitrary   c. derivative   d. astute   e. colloquial

2. The young writer worked _____ to create a style that would not be labeled as in any way based on those of other writers.

   a. divergently   b. disputatiously   c. cordially
   d. diligently   e. ambivalently

3. In Herman Melville's nineteenth-century short story "Bartleby, The Scrivener," Bartleby is a scrivener (a professional copyist) who seems to have a _____ to work; when asked to begin work, his reply is, "I would prefer not to."

   a. diligence   b. decorum   c. disinclination   d. digression   e. dissent

4. Most scientists _____ the possibility of faster-than-light travel on the grounds that it would violate the laws of nature.

    a. disclose   b. disdain   c. document   d. disperse   e. dismiss

5. The two leaders of the uprising against the government returned to their headquarters by _____ routes after the police ordered the protesters to _____ .

    a. disputatious.....dismiss
    b. divergent.....disperse
    c. discriminating.....discount
    d. derivative.....deplore
    e. divergent.....disclose

6. We _____ the incredible information that Jim had given us because he refused to _____ its source.

    a. deprecated.....discount
    b. deplored.....articulate
    c. compiled.....attribute
    d. discounted.....disclose
    e. censured.....concede

7. The research paper was regarded with _____ by scholars because its author had not carefully _____ each step of his research.

    a. diligence.....disdained
    b. degradation.....disclosed
    c. disdain.....documented
    d. depravity.....dismissed
    e. disinclination.....documented

8. Justice Smith is the most _____ judge on the appeals court; he _____ more rulings than any other judge.

    a. divergent.....documents
    b. disputatious.....dissents from
    c. discriminating.....discloses
    d. derivative.....discounts
    e. discriminating.....disdains

dogmatic

having or stating
opinions without proof

Picture this:
dog mat tick

UNIT 10

Dogmatic views from a *dog mat tick*.

■ A good book reviewer is flexible and not *dogmatic* in his or her views about what makes a book worthwhile.

■ A good scientist can't be *dogmatic* in evaluating evidence.

■ One goal of education is to make people less *dogmatic* and more open to different viewpoints.

duplicity

(doo PLIS ih tee)

deliberate deceptiveness

Picture this:
do please city

"*Do please* come to our lovely *city*,"
says Mayor *Duplicity*.

■ Joan has such a reputation for *duplicity* that we don't believe her even when what she says sounds as though it may be true.

■ The thief used *duplicity* to gain entry into the bank: he posed as a telephone repairman.

■ The spy was a mole; she used *duplicity* to gain the trust of members of the intelligence service of the foreign government in order to infiltrate it.

eclectic

composed of elements
drawn from diverse sources

Picture this:
electric

An *eclectic* collection at *Electric* Connection.

■ Lionel has an *eclectic* collection of model trains from all over the world.

■ The works of the writer Isaac Asimov demonstrate that he had remarkably *eclectic* interests; they cover practically every subject imaginable, from Shakespeare to nuclear physics.

■ Dr. McAllister owns an *eclectic* collection of art from every continent.

egotism

(EE go tiz um)

excessive self-importance;
conceit

Picture this:
E goat is him

The main concern of *E goat is him*self.
What *egotism*!

■ A good definition of growing up is losing your *egotism* and becoming more concerned about the needs of other people.

■ It could be hard to avoid *egotism* if you get straight As, have the lead in the school play, received a perfect score on the SAT, and have been selected for the all-state basketball team.

■ Some people are so *egotistical* that they hardly listen to what other people say, preferring instead to talk almost constantly.

elated

overjoyed;
in high spirits

Picture this:
eel ate Ted

Elated swimmers swam as the *eel ate Ted*.

■ The new author was *elated* to see her first book in print.

■ I was *elated* when my son phoned me to say that his wife had delivered a healthy baby girl.

■ The members of our debating team were *elated* when they won the state high school debating championship.

elegy

poem or song
expressing grief

Picture this:
a ledge he

On *a ledge*, *he* delivers an *elegy*.

■ Deeply saddened by the death of his young son, the poet Ben Jonson wrote an *elegy* to him.

■ P. B. Shelley's poem "Adonais" is an *elegy* mourning the death of John Keats at the age of twenty-five.

■ One of the great *elegies* in American literature is Walt Whitman's "When Lilacs Last in the Dooryard Bloom'd," a moving poem for President Abraham Lincoln.

(ih LOO siv)	elusive

hard to grasp; tending
to evade capture

Picture this:
a loose sieve*

"Hey you sieve, get back here!
There's gold in this here river!"

A loose sieve being *elusive*.

■ My brother, an enthusiastic surfer, goes out to the ocean
with his board every weekend in search of the *elusive*
"perfect wave."

■ Evidence for the existence of life outside of Earth has
proved *elusive*.

■ "Alley Cat" Al is an *elusive* fellow; first he escaped from
police custody, then he eluded a statewide manhunt.

* A *sieve* is an instrument with a meshed bottom. It is used to separate
coarse from fine loose matter.

embellish

(em BEL ish)

adorn; ornament;
add fictitious detail

Picture this:
Em bell

VOTE FOR THE DISH
THAT'S DISPLAYED THE BEST

EM'S
HOT DOG
BELL

Em's *bell* is *embellished* with relish.

■ Sarah *embellished* her living room with vases she had collected in her travels all over the world.

■ According to a recent survey, nearly half of all job applicants admit to *embellishing* their qualifications.

■ A journalist should not *embellish* a story to make it more interesting to the reader.

(em YOO layt)	emulate

imitate; strive to
equal or excel

Picture this:
Em you're late

"*Em, you're late*! Must you *emulate* girls
who make their dates wait?"

■ In Aesop's fable "The Tortoise and the Hare," the reader
is asked to *emulate* the tortoise; the lesson is, "Slow and
steady wins the race."

■ Jim's mother wanted her son to *emulate* his father Jumbo
Jim in all but one area—his tendency to overeat.

■ After Sharon finishes her medical training, she plans to
emulate her father and become a general practitioner in
a rural area.

endorse

(en DORS)

approve;
support

Picture this:
end horse

"That *end horse* looks good. I'll *endorse* it."

■ Senator Cash was *endorsed* by all the major newspapers.

■ After the principal *endorsed* the student council's plans for the graduation ceremony, our committee was able to go ahead with our planning for the event.

■ The English department examined the available SAT preparation books carefully; then they *endorsed* several they felt to be of sound educational value.

(EN mih tee)	enmity

ill will;
hatred

Picture this:
N mitt he

The *N mitt he* wears causes *enmity*.

■ A feud within a family sometimes causes greater *enmity* than one between people who aren't related.

■ The U.S. Civil War caused great *enmity* between the North and the South.

■ No *enmity* exists between the two rivals for the middleweight boxing championship, but each boxer does have a healthy respect for the skills of the other.

ephemeral

(ih FEM ur ul)

short-lived;
fleeting

Picture this:
a fem mural

I can explain it. You see, it's *ephemeral* art.

EPHEMERAL SCHOOL of FEM ART

A fem mural that's *ephemeral*.

- Most of the writing that appears in newspapers is *ephemeral*.

- In comparison to the billions of years that the universe has existed, the life of each living thing seems *ephemeral*.

- Much slang is *ephemeral*, but some words—such as *phony*—become part of standard English.

Memory Check 10
Match each word and its link to the corresponding definition.

dogmatic
1. **dog mat tick** __

egotism
2. **E goat is him** __

elated
3. **eel ate Ted** __

elegy
4. **a ledge he** __

elusive
5. **a loose sieve** __

embellish
6. **Em bell** __

emulate
7. **Em you're late** __

endorse
8. **end horse** __

enmity
9. **N mitt he** __

ephemeral
10. **a fem mural** __

eclectic
11. **electric** __

duplicity
12. **do please city** __

a. ill will; hatred
b. hard to grasp
c. imitate
d. poem or song expressing grief
e. excessive self-importance; conceit
f. adorn; ornament

g. short-lived; fleeting
h. overjoyed; in high spirits
i. approve; support
j. composed of elements drawn from diverse sources
k. having or stating opinions without proof
l. deliberate deceptiveness

Showtime 10
Fill in the blanks in the following sentences with the word or set of words that best fits the meaning of the sentence as a whole.

1. Some people are _____ in their views and refuse to consider the opinions of others.

    a. articulate   b. eclectic   c. disputatious   d. dogmatic   e. ephemeral

2. One judge on the appeals court disagreed with the majority opinion because she believed that the police had used _____ to obtain a confession.

    a. duplicity   b. aversion   c. diligence   d. egotism   e. ascendancy

3. Most religions teach that we should turn our attention from the _____ to the eternal.

    a. elegy   b. ephemeral   c eclectic   d. divergent   e. enmity

4. John's interests are _____ , ranging from art to electronics.

    a. ascetic   b. autonomous   c. eclectic   d. antediluvian   e. ephemeral

5. _____ grew between the directors of the rival companies after one of them _____ a plan to take over the other company.

    a. Enmity.....beguiled
    b. Egotism.....endorsed
    c. Enmity.....endorsed
    d. Antagonism.....appeased
    e. Apprehension.....deplored

6. After his good friend died, the poet wrote a (an) _____ to her; although the poem _____ her accomplishments a little, it gave a generally accurate picture of her life.

    a. elegy.....embellished
    b. accolade.....belied
    c. artifact.....embellished
    d. poem.....censured
    e. elegy.....endorsed

7. The scientist was _____ when he found the _____ evidence he had been seeking for ten years to confirm the truth of his theory.

    a. elusive.....comprehensive
    b. cursory.....elusive
    c. conciliatory.....comprehensive
    d. elated.....elusive
    e. elated.....capricious

8. Although he has many traits that can be admired and even _____ , his _____ is not one of them.

    a. debilitated.....complacency
    b. emulated.....diligence
    c. emulated.....egotism
    d. acknowledged.....decorum
    e. censured.....duplicity

equivocal

unclear in meaning;
intentionally misleading

Picture this:
equally vocal

UNIT 11

The *equivocal* candidates are *equally vocal*.

■ Debaters normally can't take an *equivocal* position if they want to win; they must take a definite position either for or against the motion proposed.

■ The judge demanded that the witness give a definite "yes" or "no" answer, but received only an *equivocal* "maybe."

■ Politicians sometimes give *equivocal* responses to questions in order to avoid having their position on an issue "pinned down."

erroneous

(ih ROH nee us)

mistaken

Picture this:
Ear Roni Us

"It says we sell *Ear Roni*? *Us*? That's *erroneous*!"

- Just because something is on the Internet doesn't mean it's true; there's a lot of *erroneous* information on the Internet.

- The belief that the distribution of wealth in America is fairly equal is *erroneous*; a recent study showed that the wealth of the richest 1 percent of the population is equal to that of the poorest 40 percent of the population.

- If your assumptions are *erroneous*, your conclusion will be incorrect, no matter how logical your reasoning is.

160

eulogy

expression
of praise

Picture this:
Yule Log* G

Mr. Claus is the nicest, kindest person in the world.

By the hearth with the glowing *Yule Log G*,
he delivers a glowing *eulogy*.

■ At the funeral of her beloved grandmother, Donna read a *eulogy* she had written to her.

■ Jim gave what might well be the shortest *eulogy* in history at his friend's funeral: "He was a pretty cool dude."

■ This biography of Abraham Lincoln isn't merely a *eulogy* to him; it examines his weaknesses as well as the qualities that made him a great president.

* A *yule log* is a large log of wood that is traditionally burned in the fireplace at Christmas.

evanescent

fleeting;
vanishing

Picture this:
even a scent

Even a scent of *Evanescent*
drives men crazy for a second.

■ Thoughts are often *evanescent*, coming into the mind for an instant and then vanishing as quickly as they came.

■ Tim joined a monastery because he believes that worldly happiness is *evanescent*, while spiritual happiness is eternal.

■ The artist is trying to capture the *evanescent* play of sunlight on the surface of the lake.

162

exalt

raise in rank or
dignity; praise

Picture this:
X Salt

X Salt is *exalted* to Superior Salt Status.

■ The combat hero was *exalted* in his hometown when he returned home from the war.

■ Having been made Bishop at the age of forty, Father Watson believed he would one day reach the *exalted* position of Cardinal.

■ When the College of Cardinals selects a Pope, he is *exalted* above all other Roman Catholics.

execute

(EK sih kyoot)

put into effect;
carry out

Picture this:
X, a cute

X, a cute letter from Texas, poised
to *execute* a triple flip.

■ Coach Harris has drilled our football team so that we can *execute* every play with precision.

■ One of the things that makes chess an interesting game is that you have to try to *execute* your own plan of attack while defending against your opponent's attack.

■ Soldiers in the ancient Greek city-state of Sparta were trained from boyhood to *execute* the plans of the leaders without question.

exemplary

serving as a model; outstanding

Picture this:
exempt Larry

"Let's *exempt Larry* from exams since he's got *exemplary* grades."

■ Although I don't agree with the book's argument, I admit that it's written in an *exemplary* manner.

■ The town council voted to recognize Ms. Miller's thirty years of *exemplary* service as town clerk with a special ceremony.

■ My English teacher said that my essay was *exemplary* and that he would read it to the class to illustrate the qualities of a good essay.

exemplify

(ig ZEM pluh fy)

serve as an example of

Picture this:
example if I

"You mean it would be a good *example if
I exemplify* the 'perfect guy'?"

■ In the eyes of many people, the astronauts *exemplify* the spirit of adventure.

■ President Theodore Roosevelt *exemplifies* for many Americans the rugged, independent man of action.

■ For many people, the spirit of the 1960s was *exemplified* at the Woodstock music festival in 1969.

(ig ZAW stiv)

exhaustive

thorough;
comprehensive

Picture this:
exhaust Steve

"Our *exhaustive* battery of tests
does not *exhaust Steve*."

- The Congressional committee completed its *exhaustive* three-month investigation into the financial crisis but failed to find any evidence of incompetence on the part of the banks.

- After an *exhaustive* review of his old tax records, Stan found a small error that he had made.

- An *exhaustive* search through my collection of reference books failed to locate the source of the quotation.

explicit

totally clear;
definite

Picture this:
X, please sit

X, please sit. I want
to talk to you about
your triple flip
that flopped.

CHEERLEADING
COACH

"*X, please sit*"—an *explicit* request.

■ Tim's parents left for a weekend at Aunt Beth's, leaving him
with *explicit* instructions: "No parties in the house. Period."

■ The Bill of Rights in the U.S. Constitution is the first *explicit*
statement of human rights in history.

■ The *explicit* meaning of the poem is clear, but its deeper,
implied meaning is much more difficult to understand.

(ik STOL)	extol

praise highly

Picture this:
X stole

"*X stole* the chocolate Xs from X Mart
and we *extol* him?"

■ My brother *extols* the virtues of camping under an open sky in a sleeping bag; I, on the other hand, prefer sleeping in a rainproof tent.

■ The family of the injured man *extolled* the doctors and nurses for the care they had given him.

■ A lot of people *extol* the pleasures of reading detective fiction, but I prefer historical fiction.

extricate   *(EK strih kayt)*

free;
disentangle

Picture this:
extra Kate

"Extra! Extra! Kate is *extricated* from the octopus!"

■ Many countries are reluctant to commit troops in foreign conflicts because it is often difficult to *extricate* them.

■ The salesman buttonholed the potential customer and gave her his long sales pitch; the poor woman couldn't *extricate* herself from the conversation without being rude.

■ The expression "Put his foot in his mouth" is often used when a person has said something embarrassing or insulting and is going to have trouble *extricating* himself gracefully from the awkward situation.

Memory Check 11

Match each word and its link to the corresponding definition.

equivocal	erroneous	eulogy
1. **equally vocal** __	2. **Ear Roni Us** __	3. **Yule Log G** __
evanescent	exalt	execute
4. **even a scent** __	5. **X Salt** __	6. **X, a cute** __
exemplary	exemplify	exhaustive
7. **exempt Larry** __	8. **example if I** __	9. **exhaust Steve** __
explicit	extol	extricate
10. **X, please sit** __	11. **X stole** __	12. **extra Kate** __

a. fleeting; vanishing
b. mistaken
c. put into effect; carry out
d. intentionally misleading
e. serving as a model; outstanding
f. disentangle

g. expression of praise
h. raise in rank or dignity
i. serve as an example of
j. totally clear; definite
k. thorough; comprehensive
l. praise highly

Showtime 11

Fill in the blanks in the following sentences with the word or set of words that best fits the meaning of the sentence as a whole.

1. It is _____ to believe that life on Earth will last forever.
   a. exemplary   b. equivocal   c. erroneous   d. explicit   e. evanescent

2. The physicists found studying the subatomic particle difficult because it was _____ .
   a. explicit   b. erroneous   c. exhaustive   d. evanescent   e. elated

3. Once a country is involved in the affairs of another country, it often finds that _____ itself is not easy.
   a. exemplifying   b. executing   c. bolstering
   d. extricating   e. extolling

4. Sal's boss _____ him in his letter of recommendation as a model employee always willing to work hard and do everything he could to ensure the success of projects he was involved with.

   a. extolled   b. extricated   c. executed   d. dismissed   e. disdained

5. Ted is a (an) _____ debater; he never takes a (an) _____ position and states his case clearly and persuasively.

   a. explicit.....contentious
   b. evanescent.....equivocal
   c. exemplary.....exhaustive
   d. bombastic.....erroneous
   e. exemplary.....equivocal

6. For the ancient Greeks, the gods were often _____ figures, _____ the best qualities of human beings.

   a. explicit.....executing
   b. exalted.....exemplifying
   c. exalted.....deploring
   d. erroneous.....exemplifying
   e. capricious.....alleviating

7. If a coach wants his team to _____ plays properly, he must make his instructions _____ .

   a. execute.....explicit
   b. advocate.....concise
   c. exalt.....exemplary
   d. acclaim.....exhaustive
   e. exemplify.....explicit

8. Jim delivered a (an) _____ to his mother that was so _____ that it lasted for over an hour.

   a. eulogy.....evanescent
   b. affirmation.....aloof
   c. antidote.....bombastic
   d. eulogy.....exhaustive
   e. degradation.....comprehensive

exuberance

joyful enthusiasm;
overflowing abundance

Picture this:
X, you bear ants

UNIT 12

"*X, you bear ants!*" he says with *exuberance*.

■ Pat could hardly contain her *exuberance* after she saw her score on the SAT; it meant she would be accepted at the college she always wanted to attend.

■ When Ted finally got the chance to play in a college football game after spending three years as backup quarterback, he played with so much *exuberance* that he inspired his team to a come-from-behind victory.

■ The book reviewer hailed the new novel as "celebrating the vitality, *exuberance*, and optimism of the American people."

facilitate

help bring about;
make less difficult

Picture this:
Fast-Ill it ate

Fast-Ill it ate to *facilitate* the illness experiment.

■ To *facilitate* the investigation into its hiring practices, the company made its personnel records available to government officials.

■ The governor's order that nonessential vehicles stay off the roads *facilitated* the movement of relief supplies into the flooded area.

■ The dictator refused to *facilitate* UN inspections of his country's nuclear weapons.

fallow

plowed but not sowed; characterized by inactivity

Picture this:
fowl low

Fowl fly *low* over a *fallow* field.

■ The field has lain *fallow* for so many years that people are beginning to wonder if its owner is planning to sell it to property developers.

■ On the first day of class, Professor Williams looked out at the faces of the freshmen in his literature class, and thought, "The minds of these students are like *fallow* fields waiting for me to plant in them the seeds of knowledge."

■ Investors are not excited by the *fallow* gold market.

falter

hesitate

Picture this:
fault her

"I really can't *fault her* if she happens to *falter*."

■ The speaker *faltered* when he came to the part of his speech in which he told his memories of his beloved wife who had died recently.

■ Our attack *faltered* soon after the enemy opened up on us with heavy artillery.

■ People with faith in human progress believe that although progress may *falter* at times, in the long run life will improve.

(fuh NAT ih siz um)	fanaticism

excessive enthusiasm;
extreme devotion to a
belief or cause

Picture this:
fanatic is Em

What a *fanatic is Em*!
Her *fanaticism* knows no bounds.

■ Moderates believe that *fanaticism* is dangerous because it divides people into opposing, often hostile, groups.

■ Miranda's *fanaticism* in imitating the dress of her favorite pop singer is beginning to worry her parents.

■ Uncle Jim is a *fanatical* follower of the Chicago Cubs baseball team; he attends nearly every game, even away games.

fastidious

difficult to please;
very careful

Picture this:
fast hideous

A *fastidious* dresser about to come
to a *fast*, *hideous* end.

■ The *fastidious* editor spent an hour considering the placement of a single comma.

■ John is a very unusual teenager—he's *fastidious* in keeping his room neat.

■ A *fastidious* housekeeper, Doris vacuums the living room carpet daily.

(FEE zuh bul)	feasible

practical

Picture this:
fees a bull

You can pay the fees to my assistant.

Pay fees to a *bull*? But *how*?

BULL AND BULL ATTORNEYS

It's not *feasible* to pay *fees* to *a bull*.

■ The outlawing of alcoholic beverages during the Prohibition period proved not to be *feasible*, and thus the Twenty-First Amendment to the Constitution was approved, repealing the Eighteenth Amendment that had banned such beverages.

■ The proposal to colonize Mars is not *feasible* because it does not include realistic plans for ensuring that the people who settle there would be able to survive in the event that supplies from Earth were disrupted.

■ The plan to guarantee every person a minimum yearly income of $30,000 is not politically *feasible*.

flagrant

conspicuously wicked;
blatant; outrageous

Picture this:
flag rant

Flagrant hostility at a *flag rant*.

■ The mayor's abuse of power became so *flagrant* that the town council decided to remove him from office.

■ In a *flagrant* violation of the school dress code, Sally wore a halter top to school yesterday.

■ Because the motorist's offense was *flagrant*, the traffic policeman had no choice but to issue a summons to him.

furtive

sneaky;
secretive

Picture this:
fir tiff

A *fir tiff* is a *furtive* affair.

- During the SAT test last week, I saw a student take a *furtive* glance at an electronic dictionary he had apparently snuck into the test center.

- The man's *furtive* behavior in the department store attracted the attention of the security guards, who suspected that he was planning to shoplift.

- The children crept *furtively* down the stairs on Christmas Eve, hoping to see their presents and perhaps even catch a glimpse of Santa Claus.

garrulous
(GAR uh lus)

talkative;
wordy

Picture this:
Gar rule us

"*Gar*, *rule us*," shouts the *garrulous* crowd.

■ The psychologist is good at encouraging reserved individuals to open up and talk about their problems; sometimes, in fact, they become so *garrulous* that she has trouble getting a word in herself.

■ The normally *garrulous* actress was speechless when it was announced that she had won the Academy Award for best actress.

■ I ran into an old friend who is so *garrulous* that I missed my dentist appointment listening to her updates on what our mutual friends have been doing.

glacial

very slowly; like a glacier; extremely cold

Picture this:
gull lay shell

Can a *gull lay* a *shell* on a *glacial* shore?

■ Negotiations on the issue are proceeding at such a *glacial* pace that there is little hope for a settlement in the foreseeable future.

■ Arctic explorers must endure *glacial* temperatures.

■ Uncle Toby completes one college credit every five years; at this *glacial* pace he'll have a degree by the time I'm a grandfather.

glutton

(GLUT n)

someone who eats and drinks excessively; having a great capacity to endure or accept a certain situation

Picture this:
glut ton

A *glutton* eats a *glut* of tuna weighing a *ton*.

- Every Sunday, Steve's Diner has a full house of *gluttons* for the all-you-can-eat buffet.

- Fast-food restaurants allow *gluttons* to satisfy their desire for food almost instantaneously.

- My girlfriend could be described as a *glutton* for shopping because she spends most of her weekends at the mall.

Memory Check 12

Match each word and its link to the corresponding definition.

furtive	glacial	exuberance
1. fir tiff __	**2. gull lay shell __**	**3. X, you bear ants __**
facilitate	fallow	falter
4. Fast-Ill it ate __	**5. fowl low __**	**6. fault her __**
fanaticism	fastidious	feasible
7. fanatic is Em __	**8. fast hideous __**	**9. fees a bull __**
flagrant	garrulous	glutton
10. flag rant __	**11. Gar rule us __**	**12. glut ton __**

a. practical
b. blatant; outrageous
c. joyful enthusiasm
d. help bring about
e. extreme devotion to a cause
f. extremely cold; very slowly

g. difficult to please
h. plowed but not sowed
i hesitate
j. secretive
k. talkative
l. someone who eats and drinks excessively

Showtime 12

Fill in the blanks in the following sentences with the word or set of words that best fits the meaning of the sentence as a whole.

1. Ms. Hansen is _____ about keeping the materials in her classroom organized.

   a. feasible   b. flagrant   c. fastidious   d. dogmatic   e. altruistic

2. I bought a new house with a big vegetable garden; however, it will have to lie _____ for a while because I don't have time for gardening right now.

   a. fallow   b. antiquated   c. abstemious   d. fastidious   e. feasible

3. Although none of his books had been praised by critics, Robert never _____ in his efforts to become a respected author.

   a. facilitated   b. conceded   c. dissented   d. censured   e. faltered

4. The normally quiet student suddenly became _____ when the teacher asked him to talk about his favorite subject, fly fishing.

   a. evanescent   b. hardy   c. gullible   d. concise   e. garrulous

5. He plays the guitar with considerable _____ ; unfortunately, however, he makes _____ mistakes that ruin his performance.

   a. composure.....feasible
   b. exuberance.....flagrant
   c. conviction.....exemplary
   d. aversion.....flagrant
   e. fanaticism.....fastidious

6. In order to _____ a compromise on the issue, the president urged each side to restrain their _____ .

   a. document.....egotism
   b. facilitate.....fanaticism
   c. endorse.....fanaticism
   d. facilitate.....ambivalence
   e. extricate.....exuberance

7. Because of the _____ cold in the area, rescue workers decided that a mission to rescue survivors from the plane that had crash-landed in Antarctica would not be _____ .

   a. comprehensive.....fastidious
   b. antediluvian.....extolled
   c. glacial.....feasible
   d. hardy.....flagrant
   e. ephemeral.....feasible

8. The _____ sneaked into the kitchen when the other guests at the party weren't looking, opened the refrigerator door, and _____ ate an entire chocolate cake.

   a. egotist.....haughtily
   b. fanatic.....cryptically
   c. charlatan.....furtively
   d. glutton.....furtively
   e. braggart.....complacently

gregarious

sociable

Picture this:
Greg Arius

UNIT 13

Greg Arius and his *gregarious* ways.

- Although human beings seem to be a generally *gregarious* species, some individuals prefer solitude.

- Some studies suggest that girls tend to be more *gregarious* than boys.

- Oliver is generally *gregarious*, but sometimes he enjoys taking some time to be alone and reflect on things.

guile

(GUY ul)

deceit; wiliness;
cunning

Picture this:
guy ill

"That *guy*? *Ill*? No, he's just
using *guile* to get us to give."

■ Unable to convince the company to hire him, Jim resorted
to *guile* and added jobs he had never had to his resume.

■ I suspected that the used car salesman was using *guile* when
he assured me that the car I was looking at had only been
driven by an old lady to church on Sundays.

■ Does a soap opera exist that doesn't have as one of the main
characters a scheming woman who uses *guile* to get what
she wants?

(GUL uh bul)	gullible

easily
deceived

Picture this:
gull-a-bull

"If you believe in the *gull-a-bull*,
you must be *gullible!*"

■ The new teacher was so *gullible* that she fell for one of the oldest excuses in the book: "Sorry, ma'am, I can't hand in my homework on time because my dog chewed it up."

■ The saying, "Never give a sucker an even break," means that one should not hesitate to take advantage of someone who is *gullible*.

■ John is definitely *gullible*: he believes the e-mail message he received saying that he was the lucky winner of a villa in France is genuine.

hamper

(HAM pur)

obstruct; make
more difficult

Picture this:
hamper

Kids, *no one's moving* until all these clothes are washed.

But you *promised* we could go canoeing this morning!

A dirty *hamper* in the camper
will *hamper* their plans.

■ My attempts to lose weight are *hampered* by the fact that my wife is an excellent cook.

■ Mandy's performance on the math test was *hampered* because her attention was focused on the handsome new student sitting next to her.

■ Coast Guard vessels trying to reach the sinking ocean liner were *hampered* by high seas in the area.

hardy

strong; sturdy

Picture this:
hard D

"Gee, this is a *hard D* to crack—talk about *hardy*!"

- The first European settlers in America had to be *hardy* to survive the harsh winters.

- A football running back must be *hardy* enough to take repeated poundings from opposing defenders.

- Health care workers are concerned about *hardy* strains of bacteria that are evolving a resistance to antibiotics.

haughtiness

pride;
arrogance

Picture this:
haw, teen S

"Haw, haw, haw—teen S displays such haughtiness!"

▪ The headwaiter in the fancy French restaurant is so *haughty* you would think that he was not a waiter but America's leading French cook.

▪ Tired of the *haughtiness* of their overbearing boss, the employees decided to complain about her to the CEO of the company.

▪ People generally expect royalty to behave with considerable *haughtiness*.

(HEED n ist)

hedonist

one who believes that pleasure is the sole aim in life

Picture this:
heed Don is

"Take *heed* of my warning. *Don is* a *hedonist!*"

- As a young man, Charles was a *hedonist,* but as he grew older he became more interested in spiritual matters.

- "Eat, drink, and be merry" is a pretty good summary of a *hedonist's* philosophy.

- Saint Augustine abandoned the *hedonistic* pursuits of his youth to pursue the spiritual life.

heresy

(HAIR uh see)

opinion contrary
to popular belief

Picture this:
Hair-a-Sea

In the little village of *Hair-a-Sea*,
it's *heresy* not to have hair.

■ The view that organized sports are a waste of time probably would be regarded as *heresy* by a majority of Americans.

■ A Ford buyer his entire life, Dad said he felt like he was committing *heresy* when he bought a Toyota last year.

■ The research suggesting that students who study at home with proper supervision perform better academically than students who attend school was regarded as *heresy* by the teachers union.

hierarchy

arrangement by
rank or standing

Picture this:
higher ark he

A *higher ark he* built in the *hierarchy* of arks.

■ Some people believe that life is organized as a *hierarchy*, with plants at the bottom, animals in the middle, and human beings at the top.

■ As Sally advanced in her career, moving steadily up the company *hierarchy*, she found that many of her colleagues envied her success.

■ Every country has a social *hierarchy* based on the status possessed by each individual.

homogeneous
(hoh muh JEE nee us)

composed of
identical parts

Picture this:
Home O genius

"O, you're a *Home O genius*! I just love
your *homogeneous* O Homes."

■ A world with a *homogeneous* population would be a pretty
boring place.

■ *Homogeneous* grouping of students has the advantage
for teachers that it allows them to tailor their lessons for
different ability groups.

■ In its early history, the United States was a relatively
homogeneous society, but as immigrants arrived from
many parts of the world, the population grew more varied.

hyperbole

exaggeration;
overstatement

Picture this:
hyper bowl

Using *hyperbole* on a *hyper bowl*.

■ "I agree with you when you say that I'm very pretty," Julie said to her boyfriend. "However, I think you're using a bit of *hyperbole* when you say I'm the prettiest girl in the *world*."

■ Writers sometimes use *hyperbole* to create "larger-than-life" characters.

■ Advertisements often use *hyperbole* to persuade people to buy products: "This revolutionary new product will change your life forever."

hypocritical

(hip uh KRIT ih kul)

pretending to be
virtuous; deceiving

Picture this:
hippo critical

I detest those
who don't do all they can
to save the environment.

A *hippo* who is *critical* being *hypocritical*.

■ Paula believes that her parents are being *hypocritical* in saying
that stealing is wrong in view of the fact that they take a
towel from every hotel they stay in when they go on vacation.

■ The bumper sticker on the vehicle in front of me telling
people to "Save the environment!" could be regarded as
hypocritical, considering that it's on a gas-guzzling SUV
spewing out a lot of pollutants that harm the environment.

■ Doris thought that her mother was being *hypocritical* in
saying that she shouldn't be married at the age of nineteen,
considering that her mother was married at eighteen.

Memory Check 13

Match each word and its link to the corresponding definition.

hedonist	hierarchy	hyperbole
1. heed Don is __	**2. higher ark he __**	**3. hyper bowl __**
hypocritical	gregarious	guile
4. hippo critical __	**5. Greg Arius __**	**6. guy ill __**
gullible	hamper	hardy
7. gull-a-bull __	**8. hamper __**	**9. hard D __**
haughtiness	heresy	homogeneous
10. haw, teen S __	**11. Hair-a-Sea __**	**12. Home O genius __**

a. person primarily seeking pleasure
b. obstruct
c. deceit; cunning
d. sociable
e. arrangement by rank
f. pretending to be virtuous
g. composed of identical parts
h. easily deceived
i. strong; sturdy
j. pride; arrogance
k. opinion contrary to popular belief
l. exaggeration

Showtime 13

Fill in the blanks in the following sentences with the word or set of words that best fits the meaning of the sentence as a whole.

1. Jill is _____ and enjoyed meeting all sorts of people at the party.
   a. aloof   b. garrulous   c. furtive   d. gullible   e. gregarious

2. If the membership of Congress is _____ , it will not accurately reflect the varied makeup of our country.
   a. homogeneous   b. colloquial   c. ascetic   d. abstract   e. gregarious

3. New presidents coming to power in Washington often use _____ in outlining what their administration will achieve.
   a. heresy   b. hierarchy   c. eulogy   d. hyperbole   e. disinclination

4. Capitalists consider it _____ to suggest that property be owned by no one but rather be shared equally by all members of the community.

    a. gregarious   b. haughty   c. heresy   d. hyperbole   e. hardy

5. That customer is really _____ ; the salesman just used a bit of _____ in the sales pitch, and she bought the product without asking any questions.

    a. hardy.....duplicity
    b. furtive.....haughtiness
    c. gullible.....guile
    d. contentious.....candor
    e. garrulous....guile

6. Being the only person _____ enough to run the marathon in less than two hours has made Bill _____ .

    a. exhaustive.....gullible
    b. hardy.....haughty
    c. haughty.....hardy
    d. discriminating.....elated
    e. glacial.....aloof

7. At least Mr. Robertson isn't a (an) _____ —he admits that he's a _____ who lives for eating and sailing his yacht.

    a. hedonist.....hypocrite
    b. adversary.....glutton
    c. charlatan.....braggart
    d. artisan.....hypocrite
    e. hypocrite.....hedonist

8. The terrorists planned to murder twelve officials at the top of the government _____ ; however, they were _____ in their attempt to carry out their plans by security officers who grew suspicious and moved the officials to a more secure location.

    a. complacency......faltered
    b. hierarchy..........hampered
    c. ascendancy.....extolled
    d. anomaly.....hampered
    e. hierarchy.....facilitated

(i kon uh KLAS tic)	iconoclastic

attacking cherished traditions

Picture this:
Ike Kono's class

UNIT 14

Iconoclastic students in *Ike Kono's class*.

- During the 1960s, many *iconoclastic* young people questioned the accepted beliefs and values of the time.

- The young art critic established her reputation by writing *iconoclastic* articles ridiculing the conservative views of other critics.

- Some *iconoclasts* in the field of education believe that the present education system should be replaced with a new one designed to meet the needs of modern society.

ignominy

(IG nuh min ee)

deep disgrace;
shame or dishonor

Picture this:
a gnome* Minnie

I'm small, but I'm certainly not ashamed of it.

*A **gnome**, **Minnie**, suffers no **ignominy**.*

■ Coach told us that there is no *ignominy* in defeat—even the 71–7 rout our team suffered—as long as we made our best effort for the entire game.

■ Because of his steadily mounting debt, the storeowner faced the *ignominy* of bankruptcy.

■ The young lieutenant's life came to an *ignominious* end when he was executed for selling military secrets to a foreign power.

* A *gnome* is a mythological dwarflike being that lives under the earth guarding treasures.

illusory

deceptive;
not real

Picture this:
a Lew sorry

I'm really sorry that I followed
this illusory dream of running for governor.
Why didn't I listen to everyone who told
me I didn't stand a chance?

ELECTION RESULTS

WALLY WINNER 8,279,291

LEW SORRY 201,227

A Lew, *sorry* for having followed
an *illusory* dream.

■ After a hard week at work coping with reality, Janet loves
to pick up a huge fantasy novel and escape into an *illusory*
land of fairies, elves, and goblins.

■ In his daydreams, Harry lived in an *illusory* world in which
he was a rich and dashing man about town.

■ After watching Josh try for twenty years to become a rock
star, his friends tried to persuade him that his dream was
illusory and that he should look for a regular job.

immutable

unchangeable

Picture this:
a mute table

An *immutable* fact:
There's no talking at *a mute table*.

- Most religions teach *immutable* values for their followers to live by.

- Science operates on the assumption that there exist laws of nature that are *immutable*.

- According to the Theory of Evolution, each species is not *immutably* fixed in its nature, but rather is in a continual process of change as it adapts to its environment.

impair

injure; hurt

Picture this:
imp* pair

The *imp pair impair* her social life.

■ Gwen's hearing is *impaired* as a result of an ear infection she had when she was a child.

■ Although the computer printer will work with the inferior ink cartridge, its ability to produce high-quality printouts will be *impaired*.

■ The movement of the throwing arm of our team's starting quarterback has been *impaired* as a result of the injury he sustained in last week's game.

* An *imp* is a child that causes mischief.

impeccable

faultless; having
no flaws

Picture this:
imp peck a bull

An *imp* tries to *peck a bull*
with *impeccable* manners.

- Although the work of the research group was *impeccable*, they were unable to identify the source of the problem.

- My fourth grade teacher insisted on *impeccable* penmanship from every student.

- The actress made sure she was dressed *impeccably* for the Academy Awards ceremonies because she knew that reporters would be out in full force, observing every detail of her appearance.

implement

put into effect

Picture this:
imp lament

They *implement* a curfew to an *imp lament*.

■ After the school board *implemented* the new policy requiring every student to write one long essay per week, the teachers protested, saying that it would be impossible for them to mark so many essays.

■ To give the workers time to adapt, the manager decided to *implement* his new production program in stages.

■ The executive branch of the U.S. government is responsible for *implementing* laws passed by the legislative branch.

impudence

(IM pyuh duns)

offensive boldness

Picture this:
imp you dance

"Imp, you dance? Your *impudence*
must be punished!"

■ The famous surgeon became angry with the young doctor for having the *impudence* to question his judgment in the case.

■ The dictator punished his adviser for his *impudence* in suggesting that more power should be given to the people.

■ The teacher ignored the *impudent* comment, knowing that responding to it would just give the student who made it the attention he was seeking.

inadvertent

unintentional; as a result of oversight; careless

Picture this:
in advert tent

In "advert tent #2" an ad man makes an *inadvertent* comment.

■ The newspaper layout person apologized to me after it was discovered that, through an *inadvertent* error, she had omitted my photograph from my column on English.

■ Sam assured Bob that although his remark could be seen as insulting, it had been *inadvertent*.

■ The traffic policeman didn't accept my excuse that I had *inadvertently* pressed the accelerator instead of the brake pedal and gave me a ticket for speeding.

incite

arouse to action

Picture this:
in sight

"We have *in sight* the guy who's
trying to *incite* a riot."

■ The lawyer's direct line of questioning was aimed to *incite* a reaction from the defendant.

■ The seaman was court-martialed for *inciting* mutiny on board the ship.

■ The rebels captured a government television station and used it to make broadcasts *inciting* a revolution.

inclusive

tending to
include all

Picture this:
in clues if

Look *in clues if* you seek *inclusive* evidence.

■ Each of the two major American political parties tries to be *inclusive*, appealing to as many types of people as possible.

■ Some people like to live in a "gated" community, separate from the larger community; I, however, prefer to live in a place that is more *inclusive*.

■ The United Nations strives to be an *inclusive* organization so that all nations are represented.

incongruous   *(in KONG groo us)*

not fitting;
absurd

Picture this:
in Congress

Incongruous behavior *in Congress.*

■ That house built in the design of a ski lodge looks *incongruous* out here in the desert.

■ It seems *incongruous* that those beautiful paintings are exhibited in a shoddy, filthy gallery.

■ The rattan furniture that looked so good in my house in Florida looks *incongruous* in my new house in Minnesota.

Memory Check 14

Match each word and its link to the corresponding definition.

impair	inadvertent	incongruous
1. imp pair __	2. in advert tent __	3. in Congress __

impudence	incite	impeccable
4. imp you dance __	5. in sight __	6. imp peck a bull __

iconoclastic	ignominy	illusory
7. Ike Kono's class __	8. a gnome Minnie __	9. a Lew sorry __

immutable	implement	inclusive
10. a mute table __	11. imp lament __	12. in clues if __

a. injure
b. unintentional
c. deceptive; not real
d. unchangeable
e. having no flaws
f. offensive boldness

g. deep disgrace; shame or dishonor
h. attacking cherished traditions
i. put into effect
j. arouse to action
k. tending to include all
l. not fitting

Showtime 14

Fill in the blanks in the following sentences with the word or set of words that best fits the meaning of the sentence as a whole.

1. The speaker's fiery speech _____ the crowd to violence.
   a. endorsed   b. deplored   c. aspired   d. incited   e. impaired

2. The teacher's _____ views on education were condemned by the conservative members of the school board.
   a. ambiguous   b. iconoclastic   c. archaic
   d. amorphous   e. hypocritical

3. Charlie decided to dress casually for the formal dinner; he regretted his decision later, however, because his _____ appearance made him feel uncomfortable all night.
   a. illusory   b. incongruous   c. impeccable
   d. iconoclastic   e. inadvertent

4. Our high school tennis team suffered the _____ of losing an exhibition match to a junior high school team.

    a. impudence   b. hyperbole   c. heresy   d. haughtiness   e. ignominy

5. The view that there exist _____ truths is regarded as _____ by many modern philosophers.

    a. ephemeral.....analogous
    b. capricious......iconoclastic
    c. dogmatic.....conciliatory
    d. concise.....hypocritical
    e. immutable.....illusory

6. The company has a (an) _____ record in the hiring of people from minority groups; it's one of the most _____ firms in the country in its hiring practices.

    a. iconoclastic.....hypocritical
    b. illusory.....evanescent
    c. discriminating.....immutable
    d. incongruous.....inadvertent
    e. impeccable.....inclusive

7. My car's ability to stop quickly in an emergency was _____ because I _____ inflated the tires to the incorrect pressure.

    a. incited.....hypocritically
    b. flagrant.....incongruously
    c. implemented....stupidly
    d. illusory.....disputatiously
    e. impaired.....inadvertently

8. Tired of the _____ of her class, Ms. Harris _____ a strict new system of punishing disrespectful students.

    a. impudence.....implemented
    b. ignominy.....documented
    c. egotism.....incited
    d. exuberance.....criticized
    e. impudence.....impaired

inconsequential

insignificant;
unimportant

Picture this:
in con sequence shall

UNIT 15

"It's *inconsequential* how we go, but *in con sequence shall* we go if you insist!"

■ "The spelling errors in my essay are *inconsequential* because they don't affect the meaning," Susie said to her English teacher.

■ Driving home from the supermarket I was involved in an accident; fortunately, however, the damage was *inconsequential*—just a minor dent in the rear bumper.

■ Richard believes so strongly that the U.S. national debt should be eliminated that he donated $1,000 to the Treasury Department; it had an *inconsequential* effect on the debt, but it made him feel a little better.

incorrigible

(in KAWR I juh bul)

not correctable; difficult to manage or control

Picture this:
encourage a bull

You really *must* slim down, you know. Just think how much more attractive you'll be after you lose 100 pounds. You'll be the **Bull of the Ball!**

Trying to *encourage a bull* to cease his *incorrigible* ways.

■ Betty is an *incorrigible* flirt—she's already chatted with every guy at the party, and it's only nine o'clock.

■ Nigel is an *incorrigible* optimist: He's flunked out of school and lost his job, and his girlfriend has dumped him; despite this, however, he's always cheerful and keeps saying that things will get better soon.

■ The prisoner's behavior had become *incorrigible*; since he refused to obey all instructions, the warden ordered that he be placed in solitary confinement.

indifferent

unmoved; unconcerned by; mediocre

Picture this:
in different

People *in different* lands being *indifferent* to each other.

- Bill is the kind of person who is *indifferent* to his surroundings; he doesn't seem to notice whether he's walking in a beautiful forest or the ugliest section of the city.

- Tired of his son's *indifferent* attitude toward schoolwork, Mr. Kilmer threatened to make him stay home all weekend to catch up with his assignments.

- The usually excellent actor gave an *indifferent* performance in the new play.

induce

(in DOOS)

persuade;
bring about

Picture this:
in deuce

Carved *in* the *deuce* was a noose
to *induce* fear in Bruce.

■ When he was eight years old, nothing could *induce* Tom to go near a girl; however, now that he's nineteen, he can't stay away from them.

■ Oliver used many strategies to *induce* Gail to marry him, including sending her a present every day.

■ A total vegetarian all his life, nothing could *induce* Jason to eat a piece of meat.

ingenious

clever;
resourceful

Picture this:
in genius

In genius we find *ingenious* ideas.

■ How often do we stop to consider the thousands of *ingenious* ideas that were the origin of the complex devices—televisions, cars, computers—that we use in our everyday lives?

■ What an *ingenious* device! It helps you to find your car keys no matter where you've put them.

■ This new detective novel has such an *ingenious* plot that it was voted best novel of the year by the detective fiction club.

inherent

firmly established
by nature or habit

Picture this:
in her aunt

In her aunt is an *inherent* need to plant.

■ Although Walter's *inherent* tendencies seem to be toward the arts, his father wants him to study science in college.

■ According to the United Nations' Universal Declaration of Human Rights, every human being possesses *inherent* political, economic, and other rights.

■ The *inherent* instability of this airplane's design makes it unsafe.

| (ih NAYT) | innate |

inborn

Picture this:
in Nate

"*In Nate* we see *innate* ability that's not being used."

■ Some people think that selfishness is *innate* in human beings.

■ Intelligence tests are designed to measure a person's *innate* ability.

■ Psychologists believe that some personality traits, such as introversion and extroversion, are to a significant degree *innate*.

innocuous

(ih NOK yoo us)

harmless; unlikely to
provoke strong emotion

Picture this:
in a queue* us

In a queue with *us* were several *innocuous* snakes.

- King, my family's German Shepherd, looks ferocious, but I assure you that he's actually *innocuous*.

- Don's illness seemed *innocuous* at first, but steadily became worse until his life was in danger.

- The fumes might appear *innocuous*—they smell pleasant enough—however, prolonged exposure to them will almost certainly harm your health.

* A *queue* is a line of people waiting their turn for something.

(in uh VAY shun)	innovation

change; introduction
of something new

Picture this:
inn ovation

How innovative!

It's a totally new idea!

The inn is so innovative that it has a skating rink on its roof.

A real *inn ovation* for this inn's *innovation*.

- The space shuttle was an *innovation* in space flight; however, some experts now believe that a return to older types of spacecraft is advisable because of the problems the shuttle has had.

- One of the great recent *innovations* in communications is e-mail.

- Ms. Chambliss won this year's teacher-of-the-year award for her *innovative* and effective approaches to conducting lessons.

instigate

provoke;
start; urge

Picture this:
inn's Tea Gate

The waiter at the *inn's Tea Gate*
instigates a tea debate.

■ The revolutionary *instigated* a rebellion among the
people by spreading rumors that the king was planning to
confiscate all private property.

■ The principal will eventually find out who *instigated* the
fight, so you might as well confess that it was you.

■ Security officials are searching for a group that it believes to
be *instigating* the overthrow of the government.

224

insularity

narrow-mindedness;
isolation

Picture this:
Inn Sue-Larry Tea

Sue and Larry live in *insularity*
drinking *Inn Sue-Larry Tea*.

■ The *insularity* of China during much of its history
caused many people in that country to be suspicious
of foreigners.

■ These native people live an *insular* existence in their remote
mountain village.

■ Europeans sometimes accuse Americans of *insularity*; they
say Americans tend to regard events occurring beyond the
borders of their country as having little relevance to them.

integrity

(in TEG rih tee)

uprightness;
wholeness

Picture this:
in tea gritty

"In . . . tea . . . gritty stuff.
She has no *integrity!"*

■ The community expects schoolteachers to be individuals of
integrity whom young people can respect.

■ Amber is a person of *integrity*; she could have kept the
$10,000 in the wallet that she found and no one would have
been the wiser; instead, she returned the wallet and the
money to their rightful owner.

■ The bank clerk was believed to be a person of *integrity*—
until it was discovered that she had withdrawn $300,000
from a customer's account and left town in the night.

Memory Check 15

Match each word and its link to the corresponding definition.

innocuous
1. **in a queue us** __

innovation
2. **inn ovation** __

inherent
3. **in her aunt** __

induce
4. **in deuce** __

indifferent
5. **in different** __

insularity
6. **Inn Sue-Larry Tea** __

innate
7. **in Nate** __

integrity
8. **in tea gritty** __

inconsequential
9. **in con sequence shall** __

incorrigible
10. **encourage a bull** __

ingenious
11. **in genius** __

instigate
12. **inn's Tea Gate** __

a. clever
b. harmless
c. unconcerned by
d. introduction of something new
e. firmly established by nature or habit
f. provoke; start

g. inborn
h. difficult to manage or control
i. persuade; bring about
j. unimportant
k. uprightness; wholeness
l. narrow-mindedness

Showtime 15

Fill in the blanks in the following sentences with the word or set of words that best fits the meaning of the sentence as a whole.

1. The principal decided to introduce strict rules to control the _____ students who refuse to behave themselves in class.

   a. incorrigible   b. innocuous   c. inconsequential
   d impaired   e. indifferent

2. Have you ever had the experience of hearing a remark that seemed _____ at the time but it later took on great importance for you?

   a. incongruous   b. inconsequential   c. indifferent
   d. inadvertent   e. inherent

3. The plan's _____ weaknesses meant that it would not be able to achieve its intended objectives.

   a. innocuous   b. inconsequential   c. inherent   d. insular   e. indifferent

4. There is some biological evidence that musical ability is to some extent
   _____ .

   a. ingenious   b. innate   c. integrity   d. inadvertent   e. incongruous

5. The scientist's _____ research led to discoveries that later helped
   engineers produce _____ in several fields.
   a. ingenious.....anomalies
   b. indifferent.....insularity
   c. inherent.....innovations
   d. impeccable.....conflagrations
   e. ingenious.....innovations

6. Nothing could _____ the people of Little Creek to give up their
   small town _____ and adopt the attitudes of city people.
   a. incite.....integrity
   b. confound.....fanaticism
   c. induce.....insularity
   d. advocate.....depravity
   e. innate.....insularity

7. The police identified a man who appeared _____ , but whom
   they believed was _____ young people to commit crimes.
   a. furtive.....inciting
   b. innocuous.....instigating
   c. ingenious.....inducing
   d. inherent.....instigating
   e. impeccable.....acclaiming

8. The lawyer's professional _____ demanded that he defend his
   client to the best of his ability even though the man's fate was a matter
   about which he was _____ .
   a. innovation.....innocuous
   b. insularity.....indifferent
   c. diligence.....equivocal
   d. egotism.....benevolent
   e. integrity.....indifferent

intimidate

frighten; coerce or inhibit by threats

Picture this:
intimate date

UNIT 16

An *intimate date* tends to *intimidate* her.

- Don't let the difficult vocabulary on the SAT *intimidate* you; if you study systematically, you can learn most of the words likely to appear on it.

- The president deployed the Seventh Fleet to *intimidate* the potentially aggressive nation.

- When the Maori warriors of New Zealand do a war dance called the haka, they *intimidate* their enemies.

intrepid

fearless

Picture this:
in trip heed*

Even the most *intrepid* explorer should,
in his *trip*, *heed* warnings.

■ An *intrepid* investor, Mr. Wilcox regularly puts a large part of his savings into high-risk stocks.

■ Only a few *intrepid* climbers have dared to scale the sheer wall of Mt. Doom.

■ Mary is *intrepid* in pursuing her dream of becoming a published writer; despite having received hundreds of rejections, she submits a new story every week.

* To *heed* is to pay careful attention to something.

ironic

happening in a way opposite to what is expected, and typically causing wry amusement because of this

Picture this:
Iron Nick

"It's *ironic* that *Iron Nick* was flattened by a load of barbells."

■ It was an *ironic* twist of fate for the greatest swimmer in Olympic history—drowning in a swimming pool.

■ Isn't it *ironic* that it was the worst student in the English class who later became a distinguished novelist?

■ It was *ironic* that now that everybody had plenty of money for food, they could not obtain food because everything had ben rationed.

jocular

(JOK yuh lur)

said or done
in jest

Picture this:
jock caller

A *jock caller* says something *jocular*.

- The young diplomat closed his tribute to the outgoing ambassador with what he intended to be a *jocular* remark about the ambassador's love of food; the ambassador, however, saw it as an insult.

- Tim's continual *jocular* comments were starting to annoy Sue: "Can't you ever be serious?" she asked.

- We were surprised to see our usually serious math teacher in a *jocular* mood, cracking jokes a mile a minute.

lament

grieve; express sorrow

Picture this:
Lamb meant

Professor *Lamb meant* to *lament*
the death of his favorite lamb in Kent.

■ "Kids today aren't as serious as we were in our day" is a *lament* that has been expressed by the older generation about the younger generation through the ages.

■ There's little point in *lamenting* the end of summer vacation—the first day of school will come around regardless.

■ In his old age, Dave *lamented* the lost opportunities of his youth.

lavish

extravagant;
wasteful

Picture this:
laugh fish

HA HA HA HEE HEE HEE HA HA HA

What do you think
of the *laugh fish?*

Laugh fish serenade them at a *lavish* feast.

■ When my company makes a million dollars, I'll invite all
my employees to a *lavish* dinner to celebrate.

■ The young couple regret their *lavish* spending on their
honeymoon trip; now they don't have enough money for
a down payment on the house they want to buy.

■ The salesman entertained his clients *lavishly*, hoping to
close the big deal with them.

linger

loiter or dawdle;
continue or persist

Picture this:
Lynn Gere

"*Lynn Gere* loves to *linger* here."

■ Most of the guests left the party at midnight, but Robin and Gwen *lingered* into morning, talking about their different philosophies of life.

■ After the funeral, the old woman *lingered* a while at her husband's grave, recalling their long life together.

■ The last cold I had *lingered* for so long I thought that I'd have it for the rest of my life.

listless

lacking in spirit
or energy

Picture this:
list-less

Lisa is *listless* because she's *"list-less."*

■ Our football team was *listless* in the first half and fell behind 28 to 7, but in the second half they came back to life and mounted a comeback.

■ We were surprised by the band's *listless* performance until we learned that the band had been touring for three months straight and its members were exhausted.

■ It's such a hot day that everyone is *listless*, just sitting around the house eating ice cream and drinking soda.

(LAWF tee)	lofty

very high

Picture this:
loft he

In a *loft he* lived—in a *lofty* mountain hideaway.

■ The United States now occupies the *lofty* position of the most powerful country in the world.

■ As a child, Clarence had the *lofty* ambition of becoming governor of our state; however, when he grew up he had to be content with a seat on the town council.

■ *Lofty* ideals are of little use unless they are put into practice.

meander
(mee AN dur)

wind or turn
in its course

Picture this:
me and her

"You'll be seeing a lot of *me and her*
as we *meander* 'round the mountain."

■ Highway 61 *meanders* for hundreds of miles through the rolling farmland of Dylan County.

■ Black Muddy River *meanders* through the valley down toward the sea.

■ Professor Barzun's lectures are remarkable; they *meander* through all the areas of history, shedding light on each of them.

mercenary

interested in
money or gain

Picture this:
myrrh scenery

A *mercenary* Moor stops to admire
the *myrrh scenery*.

■ The investor's motive in building a resort in the poor
country isn't entirely *mercenary*; he believes that a resort
will bring employment that will help the local people.

■ Responding to critics who complained that he seemed to
write for *mercenary* rather than artistic motives, the writer
replied, "Even writers have to eat and pay the mortgage."

■ Although offers of free services on the Internet are often
attractive, there is often a *mercenary* motive behind them:
if you sign up for a free service, you're more likely to later
sign up for a service that you have to pay for.

meticulous

(muh TIK yuh lus)

painstaking;
excessively careful

Picture this:
met tickle us

"Her behavior was far from *meticulous*.
Whenever we *met*, she would *tickle us*!"

■ The novelist planned the plot of her novel in *meticulous* detail.

■ Mr. Tan's lawn is *meticulous*; he spends two hours every weekend working on it.

■ Herb's *meticulous* preparation for the SAT was rewarded with a perfect score.

Memory Check 16
Match each word and its link to the corresponding definition.

intimidate	intrepid	ironic
1. **intimate date** __	2. **in trip heed** __	3. **Iron Nick** __
jocular	lament	lavish
4. **jock caller** __	5. **Lamb meant** __	6. **laugh fish** __
linger	listless	lofty
7. **Lynn Gere** __	8. **list-less** __	9. **loft he** __
meander	mercenary	meticulous
10. **me and her** __	11. **myrrh scenery** __	12. **met tickle us** __

a. happening in a way opposite to what is expected
b. lacking in spirit or energy
c. frighten; coerce or inhibit by threats
d. grieve; express sorrow
e. extravagant
f. interested in money or gain

g. loiter; persist
h. said or done in jest
i. wind or turn in its course
j. very high
k. fearless
l. painstaking

Showtime 16
Fill in the blanks in the following sentences with the word or set of words that best fits the meaning of the sentence as a whole.

1. Not many students _____ at the test site after the SAT was finished; everyone wanted to get back home and relax.
   a. intimidated   b. meandered   c. lingered   d. extricated   e. aspired

2. It's _____ that the author of the recently published book about how to lose weight didn't succeed in losing weight herself.
   a. indifferent   b. ingenious   c. innocuous   d. incorrigible   e. ironic

3. The teachers in the town were accused of being _____ when they asked for a raise.
   a. mercenary   b. meticulous   c. lofty   d. lavish   e. ironic

4. A (an) _____ investigation by the police uncovered a clever, well-hidden scheme to defraud retirees out of their life savings.

    a. mercenary b. listless c. meticulous d. ironic e. jocular

5. Joe was so _____ by the immensity of his task—learning 3,500 words for the SAT—that he became _____ and couldn't concentrate on learning the words.

    a. intimidated.....jocular
    b. instigated.....ambivalent
    c. elated.....indifferent
    d. impaired.....fastidious
    e. intimidated.....listless

6. Marsha is _____ in her pursuit of her _____ goal of becoming the first woman president of the United States; she has overcome every obstacle in her way so far and will be nominated by her party for the office next year.

    a. assiduous.....inherent
    b. incorrigible.....lofty
    c. lofty.....intrepid
    d. intrepid.....lofty
    e. ironic.....exemplary

7. The two friends _____ through the streets of the city, talking and _____ the fact that they had not done anything to prepare for the SAT test they were taking the next morning.

    a. dispersed.....acclaiming
    b. meandered.....lamenting
    c. beguiled.....lamenting
    d. coalesced.....acknowledging
    e. lingered.....deploring

8. Heather apologized _____ to her friend Wendy for insulting her, but knew that she still harbored resentment and that it would be a long time before they would return to their _____ banter.

    a. ironically.....innocuous
    b. listlessly.....jocular
    c. intrepidly.....lofty
    d. erroneously.....garrulous
    e. lavishly.....jocular

miserly

stingy

Picture this:
Miser Lee

UNIT 17

Miser Lee—a miserly old man.

■ Most of the year Dad is *miserly* when it comes to letting us buy luxuries, but at Christmas he drops the Scrooge routine and lets us buy pretty much whatever we want.

■ Our football coach, Mr. Edwards, is *miserly* in handing out praise; after we beat the top-ranked team in the state 58 to 0, he just said, "That was a good game, boys."

■ Considered the most *miserly* boss in town, Mr. King surprised us when he gave us all a 20 percent raise.

mitigate

moderate
in intensity

Picture this:
mitt a gate

They drop his *mitt* by *a gate* to *mitigate* his anger.

■ The government provided food subsidies to *mitigate* the effects of the depression on the poor.

■ Most medicines that can be bought over-the-counter only *mitigate* the effects of an ailment; they don't cure the ailment itself.

■ The judge decided that because of the *mitigating* circumstances of the case he would not impose the most severe sentence possible.

(muh ROHS)	morose

sad; gloomy

Picture this:
more rose

Morose Mary needs *more rose*.

■ The ancient Greek philosopher Socrates believed that a person shouldn't become *morose*, even when facing his or her own death.

■ The mood in the room after news of the tragedy was *morose*.

■ She becomes *morose* when she thinks about her failed marriage.

picture made of colorful
small inlaid tiles;
something that resembles a
mosaic

Picture this:
most say ick

Most say "ick" when they see Moe's icky mosaic.

- In the Roman Empire, floors were decorated with *mosaics* made up of marble slabs of various colors.

- The detective pieced together the clues at the scene of the crime until they formed a *mosaic* that gave him a clear picture of how all the events led to the crime.

- The church of Hagia Sophia in Istanbul, Turkey is famous for its beautiful gold *mosaics*.

(mun DAYN)	mundane

worldly as opposed to spiritual; everyday; concerned with the commonplace

Picture this:
Monday

A *mundane Monday*.

■ Professor Pascal has little time for the *mundane* business of running her laboratory; she leaves that to her assistant so that she can concentrate on research.

■ The English teacher asked his students to record not the *mundane* details of their lives but rather their observations and reflections.

■ A talented writer can make even a *mundane* topic like brushing your teeth or mowing the lawn interesting.

munificent

(myoo NIF ih sunt)

very generous

Picture this:
Moon, if I sent

"*Moon, if I sent* you an atmosphere
it would be a *munificent* act."

- The *munificent* businessman donated five million dollars to the school building fund.

- Andrew Carnegie, a rich and *munificent* nineteenth-century industrialist, established over 2,800 public libraries in the United States.

- The poor farmer is remarkably *munificent*; although he can hardly afford to feed his own family, he never turns away a stranger in need of a meal.

(nuh FAR ee us)	nefarious

very wicked

Picture this:
Neff ferry us

"He can't have The *Neff ferry us* over—
there's a *nefarious* spy on board!"

■ The terrorists' *nefarious* plan to spy on the elementary school was uncovered through alert police work.

■ The actor, famous for his portrayals of *nefarious* characters, longed to play the "good guy" for a change.

■ The hackers' *nefarious* plan was to break into computers in banks around the country and make them crash, causing chaos in the economy.

nonchalance (non shuh LAHNS)

indifference; casual
lack of concern

Picture this:
non shell lance*

"Shell lance or *non shell lance*?" he asks
with *nonchalance*.

■ After being nearly "beaned" by an inside fastball, Luke got
up, dusted himself off, and with complete *nonchalance*,
delivered the game-winning hit on the next pitch.

■ Dad acted *nonchalant* about his promotion to vice-
president of the company, but we all knew that he was
actually very excited about it.

■ An appearance of *nonchalance* is required for anyone who
wants to be considered "cool."

* A *lance* is a spearlike weapon with a long shaft and a sharp metal head.

notoriety

ill fame (being known
widely and unfavorably)

Picture this:
Noto Riot he

For his part in the *Noto Riot*, *he* gained
instant *notoriety*.

- The student gained *notoriety* on campus for cheating on
her final exams.

- Our football team's left defensive end has gained *notoriety*
around the conference for his dirty play.

- The writer received *notoriety* in the literary world when
it was discovered that he had copied most of the ideas
for his best-selling book from a long-forgotten work by
another author.

novelty

something new;
newness

Picture this:
Novel Tea

It's a special infusion of *orange pekoe, bergamot, creativity, Darjeeling,* and *literary sensibility.* People are coming in and drinking my tea and churning out novels like crazy.

NOVEL TEA HOUSE

BILL'S NOVELS

JEAN'S NOVELS

FRED'S NOVELS

NOVEL TEA

Novel Tea is a *novelty* that sparks creativity.

■ When automobiles were first introduced, they were considered a *novelty*, but they soon became considered a normal, necessary part of life by most people.

■ The *novelty* of college life wore off after a few months, and Alice settled into a routine of going to her classes and then the library to study and do research.

■ After receiving Ds and Fs on his English essays all year, it was a *novelty* for Larry to receive a B.

nurture

nourish; educate;
foster

Picture this:
near shore

On the *near shore* they *nurture* narcissi.

■ In some families, the mother has the primary responsibility
for *nurturing* the children.

■ My mathematics teacher *nurtures* mathematical talent in
students by giving them encouragement and guidance.

■ The newspaper editor carefully *nurtured* the talent of her
writers, helping them to steadily become better at
their craft.

obliterate

destroy completely

Picture this:
Ob Letter Eight

"We have destroyed the alien spacecraft."

In *Ob Letter Eight*, Oblantis *obliterates* aliens.

■ Rising sea levels threaten to *obliterate* many of the island nations of the world.

■ The meteor was *obliterated* when it collided with the Moon.

■ After her divorce, Tammy *obliterated* everything she had that reminded her of her ex-husband.

Memory Check 17

Match each word and its link to the corresponding definition.

novelty	obliterate	miserly
1. **Novel Tea** __	2. **Ob Letter Eight** __	3. **Miser Lee** __
mitigate	morose	mosaic
4. **mitt a gate** __	5. **more rose** __	6. **most say ick** __
mundane	munificent	nefarious
7. **Monday** __	8. **Moon, if I sent** __	9. **Neff ferry us** __
nonchalance	nurture	notoriety
10. **non shell lance** __	11. **near shore** __	12. **Noto Riot he** __

a. nourish; educate
b. very wicked
c. very generous
d. stingy
e. ill fame
f. sad; gloomy

g. everyday
h. destroy completely
i. moderate in intensity
j. something new
k. casual lack of concern
l. picture made of colorful tiles

Showtime 17

Fill in the blanks in the following sentences with the word or set of words that best fits the meaning of the sentence as a whole.

1. In order to _____ the negative effects of the recession on the population, Congress passed a law increasing unemployment benefits.
   a. intimidate   b. obliterate   c. nurture   d. mitigate   e. instigate

2. American society is sometimes compared to a _____ made up of people of nearly every culture and race on Earth.
   a. mercenary   b. mosaic   c. nonchalance   d. novelty   e. notoriety

3. The mechanic gained _____ in the town when a newspaper featured him in a report about mechanics who cheat customers on car repairs.
   a. novelty   b. lament   c. nonchalance   d. notoriety   e. integrity

4. The dictator ordered all records of previous democratic rule in the country be _____ .

    a. mitigated   b. lamented   c. meandered   d. nurtured   e. obliterated

5. The writer became so _____ after his manuscript was rejected that he had trouble attending to the _____ tasks of everyday life.

    a. debilitated.....innocuous
    b. meticulous.....morose
    c. miserly.....nefarious
    d. listless.....mercenary
    e. morose.....mundane

6. The teachers in our town were accused by some people of being _____ ; the teachers, in turn, said that the school board was being _____ considering that plenty of funds were available and that they were only asking for enough of a pay raise to cover the increase in the cost of living.

    a. mercenary.....miserly
    b. miserly.....mercenary
    c. nefarious.....mercenary
    d. morose.....meticulous
    e. meticulous.....miserly

7. A _____ investigation by the police uncovered a _____ scheme to defraud the company.

    a. miserly.....mercenary
    b. meticulous.....nefarious
    c. mundane.....novel
    d. munificent.....miserly
    e. nefarious.....mercenary

8. The _____ with which the _____ computer tycoon wrote out a check for two million dollars for the disaster relief fund was astonishing.

    a. mosaic.....nefarious
    b. munificence.....miserly
    c. nonchalance.....munificent
    d. notoriety....altruistic
    e. munificence.....mercenary

oblivion

obscurity;
forgetfulness

Picture this:
Ob live eon

UNIT 18

*Ob live*d an *eon* before Oblantis fell into *oblivion*.

■ The scholar's careful research discovered a long-lost manuscript by William Shakespeare, thus rescuing it from *oblivion*.

■ Very few writers are remembered past their own generation; most fall into *oblivion*, completely forgotten by both readers and critics.

■ Some people believe that after a person dies there is *oblivion*.

obscure

indistinct; not
easily understood

Picture this:
Ob's Cure

You mean Ob had found a cure
for the human condition?

Ob's Cure

TO FIX YOUR CONDITION AND TRANSFORM YOU INTO A HIGHER ENTITY

Yes, dear, but
unfortunately
it was lost
when Oblantis
fell into oblivion.

Ob's Cure lost in *obscure* times.

■ The *obscure* writer wrote twenty books before finally capturing the attention of the reading public.

■ The meaning of this poem is so *obscure* that even the best critics disagree about it.

■ The poet made a reference to an *obscure* fourteenth-century artist that only an art historian would be familiar with.

258

obstinate

stubborn; hard to control or treat

Picture this:
Ob stun eight

You guys were so *obstinate*, I had to use level 10 to knock you out.

OB SUPREME ROD

How many aliens did *Ob stun*?
Eight, exactly eight *obstinate* aliens.

■ Tim is *obstinate* about one thing: he refuses to go out with his friends until he's completed all of his homework.

■ My car is *obstinate*; it refused to start, even though I had tuned the engine a week earlier.

■ The *obstinate* child clung to her mother, wailing and refusing to get on the bus and go to nursery school.

ominous

(OM uh nus)

threatening

Picture this:
O' Minus

"Beware *O' Minus*" reads the *ominous* message.

- It was an *ominous* sign when the two countries broke off diplomatic relations and mobilized their military forces.

- The defendant became worried as the jury filed back into the courtroom after their deliberations, all with *ominous* grim expressions on their faces.

- The economic indicators are *ominous*—a falling stock market, high unemployment, and zero growth.

opportunist

one who sacrifices principles for gain by taking advantage of circumstances

Picture this:
a port Tunis

At *a port* near *Tunis*, an *opportunist* waits.

■ During wartime, *opportunists* often profit from shortages of important materials, stockpiling them and later selling them at high prices.

■ After the town's water supply became contaminated, *opportunists* began selling bottled water at triple the regular price.

■ The lawyer is an *opportunist*; she approaches people injured in car accidents and asks them if they'd like her help in suing other parties involved.

opulence

(OP yuh luns)

extreme wealth;
luxuriousness; abundance

Picture this:
opal* lance**

"An *opal lance*? Such *opulence* in this palace!"

■ Even though he's rich, the billionaire lives simply with none of the *opulence* usually associated with great wealth.

■ Harry decided to show off his *opulence* by buying a private jet and expensive works of art.

■ In this city, you can walk in a few minutes from a street lined with *opulent* houses to a street with nothing but rundown tenements.

* *Opal* is a shining, sparkling gemstone.
** A *lance* is a spearlike weapon with a long shaft and a sharp metal head.

orator

public speaker

Picture this:
oar rater

"The *oar rater* thinks he's an *orator*!"

■ Although she was not a particularly good *orator*, people listened closely to Ruth's talk because she spoke about her difficult experiences with complete honesty.

■ In the age of television, a politician needs fewer of the skills of the traditional *orator* and more of those of a popular television personality.

■ The *orator* held the crowd spellbound with her fascinating speech and exciting way of speaking.

ornate

(or NAYT)

excessively or
elaborately decorated

Picture this:
oar Nate

The *oar Nate* made was very *ornate*.

■ Taste in art today tends to prefer straightforward,
unadorned designs as opposed to designs that are *ornate*.

■ Modern readers tend to prefer writing that is simple and
direct to writing that is *ornate*.

■ We marveled at the *ornately* carved chair created by the
master furniture maker.

pacifist

one opposed to
force; anti-militarist

Picture this:
pass a fist

A *pacifist* must *pass a fist*.

■ A group of *pacifists* protested peacefully against the war.

■ *Pacifists* in Hitler's Germany could do little to prevent that
country's conquest of many of its European neighbors.

■ One of the best-known *pacifist* churches is the Society of
Friends, also called the Quakers.

parody

(PAIR uh dee)

a literary or musical work that imitates the style of another work for comic effect or ridicule

Picture this:
pair ready

"Is the *pair ready* for their *parody*?"

■ Our English teacher asked us to write a *parody* of a scene from *Julius Caesar*.

■ The book *The Hitch-hiker's Guide to the Galaxy* by Douglas Adams can be read as a *parody* of science fiction novels.

■ The governor took the *parody* done of one of his press conferences in surprisingly good humor considering how foolish it made him appear.

partisan

one-sided; prejudiced;
committed to a party

Picture this:
party sin

Party sin #1: Inviting a *partisan* to your party.

■ Although all the new appointees to the state supreme court belonged to his own political party, the governor claimed that *partisan* politics played no part in his selection process.

■ The moderator tried hard to not be *partisan* during the debate, but several times it was obvious that he favored the candidate of one party over that of the other party.

■ The president addressed the nation, asking people to put aside *partisan* differences and work together.

paucity

scarcity

Picture this:
Paw City

In *Paw City*, there's no *paucity* of people with paws.

■ According to the law of supply and demand, a *paucity* of a good will cause its price to increase.

■ Despite having a *paucity* of natural resources, Singapore has become one of the wealthiest countries in the world.

■ In some cities, such as New York and San Francisco, there is a *paucity* of eligible men for women to marry.

Memory Check 18

Match each word and its link to the corresponding definition.

oblivion	ominous	ornate
1. Ob live eon __	2. O' Minus __	3. oar Nate __
opulence	parody	opportunist
4. opal lance __	5. pair ready __	6. a port Tunis __
paucity	obscure	pacifist
7. Paw City __	8. Ob's Cure __	9. pass a fist __
obstinate	orator	partisan
10. Ob stun eight __	11. oar rater __	12. party sin __

a. excessively decorated
b. extreme wealth
c. stubborn
d. scarcity
e. obscurity; forgetfulness
f. a literary or musical work that imitates the style of another work for comic effect or ridicule

g. one who sacrifices principles for gain by taking advantage of circumstances
h. indistinct; not easily understood
i. prejudiced
j. public speaker
k. one opposed to force
l. threatening

Showtime 18

Fill in the blanks in the following sentences with the word or set of words that best fits the meaning of the sentence as a whole.

1. The artist presented his _____ masterpiece.
   a. partisan   b. ominous   c. innate   d. obstinate   e. ornate

2. The poem is so _____ that scholars can't agree on what it means.
   a. morose   b. mundane   c. partisan   d. ominous   e. obscure

3. The villain in the movie was _____ ; you could tell he was going to do something bad the first chance he could.
   a. partisan   b. miserly   c. ominous   d. ornate   e. obstinate

4. The governor is _____ in her refusal to sign the bill unless more evidence is given to show that it will benefit everyone in the state.

    a. ominous b. obscure   c. partisan   d. ornate   e. obstinate

5. There is no _____ of millionaires in Monte Carlo; the _____ of the houses there is amazing.

    a. paucity.....pacifist

    b. parody.....oblivion

    c. partisan.....parody

    d. paucity...opulence

    e. partisan.....paucity

6. The _____ carefully _____ his relationship with all whom he meets, gaining their trust so that later he can take advantage of any opportunity to cheat them.

    a. orator.....laments

    b. opportunist.....nurtures

    c. pacifist.....lavishes

    d. parody.....obliterates

    e. opportunist.....parodies

7. It was a (an) _____ for the film class to watch a funny _____ after they had watched so many films that took themselves so seriously.

    a. novelty...parody

    b. parody.....novelty

    c. opportunist.....parody

    d. paucity.....oblivion

    e. novelty.....pacifist

8. The _____ was a (an) _____ ; she argued that the only way that lasting peace could be achieved was through governments renouncing the use of war to achieve their objectives.

    a. pacifist.....opportunist

    b. orator.....pacifist

    c. parody.....partisan

    d. orator.....novelty

    e. mercenary.....pacifist

penury

severe poverty;
stinginess

Picture this:
pen Yuri

UNIT 19

In the *pen*, *Yuri* lived in *penury*.

■ The expense of the long legal battle will reduce both sides to *penury* unless they arrive at a settlement soon.

■ During the Great Depression of the early twentieth century, some millionaires lost so much money that they had to live in *penury*.

■ Though he had been reduced to *penury* by the bankruptcy of his business, Mr. Ford remained confident that he would soon recover and be wealthy again.

peripheral

(puh RIF ur ul)

outer;
marginal

Picture this:
pear for all

"There's a *pear for all* on the *peripheral* pear trees!"

■ A good manager must be able to decide which tasks must be done very soon and which ones can be put off to later because they're *peripheral*.

■ Because the negotiator believed that it was important to build trust between the parties in the dispute, she encouraged them to settle *peripheral* issues before moving on to more important issues.

■ Scientists must focus on the essential aspects of what they're studying, excluding anything that is *peripheral*.

perpetuate

make something last;
preserve from extinction

Picture this:
purr pet you ate

My dad ate
our purr pet,
you know.

Hey, did you
hear about how
my dad ate our
purr pet?

"They *perpetuate* that crazy tale
about the *purr pet you ate*."

■ The untrue rumor was *perpetuated* by people who heard it
and then passed it on because it sounded so amazing.

■ The neighborhood bully did everything he could to
perpetuate the myth that no one could beat him in a fight.

■ Many types of animals are becoming so few in number that
there's a danger that they will not be able to *perpetuate*
their species.

phenomena

(fih NOM uh nuh)

observable facts; subjects
of scientific investigation

Picture this:
fin omen—ahhh!

Now it's a rare *fin omen!*
Ahhh! This all means we're going
to have a great catch!

AHHH AHHH AHHH

"Now it's a *fin omen—ahhh!*—
rare *phenomena!*"

■ Scientists must keep accurate records of the *phenomena*
they study.

■ Physicists study the *phenomena* of nature in order to
discover their underlying laws.

■ Scientists use instruments such as telescopes and microscopes
to extend the range of human senses so that they can study
phenomena in nature more comprehensively.

pithy

concise; meaningful;
substantial; meaty

Picture this:
pit he

Outsmarted by a pithosaurus!

In the *pit*, *he* makes a *pithy* remark.

■ The eighteenth-century writer Samuel Johnson is famous
for his *pithy* remarks, such as "No man but a blockhead
ever wrote, except for money."

■ In this age of the politics of the "sound bite"—a short
statement that can be played on television for a very short
period of time—it is important for a candidate to be able
to come up with *pithy* statements that express his or her
views in a few words.

■ Try putting a *pithy* quotation from a well-known person in
your essay to capture your reader's interest.

placate (PLAY kayt)

pacify;
lessen the anger of

Picture this:
play Cate

In the *play*, *Cate* must *placate* an angry mob.

■ To *placate* the angry customer, the store manager gave her a $100 gift voucher.

■ After Bob's father threatened to take away the keys to his car if he didn't study for the SAT, Bob *placated* him by studying for an hour.

■ Nigel could see that *placating* his boss was not going to be easy; she had a right to be angry with him for his carelessness in forgetting to call their most important client.

polemical

aggressive in verbal attack; disputatious; relating to argument or controversy

Picture this:
polar Mick call

A *polemical polar Mick call.*

■ Rather than reasonably discussing issues of concern to voters, the speakers in the forum gave *polemical* speeches attacking the views of their opponents.

■ Senator Smith had been told that the debate would be a reasonable discussion of the issue, but her opponent launched into a *polemical* speech denouncing her position.

■ The candidate for office closed the debate with these words: "I had hoped this would be a fair evaluation of the political situation, but instead my opponent has used it as an opportunity for *polemical* attacks on me."

ponderous

(PON dur us)

unwieldy from weight;
labored and dull

Picture this:
pond her Russ

At the *pond, her Russ* makes a *ponderous* proposal.

- Frequently, and for obvious reasons, the refrigerator is the most *ponderous* appliance in the house to move.

- To take his mind off *ponderous* matters of state for a while, the president went to see a movie.

- The amateur comedian was so *ponderous* in his delivery that by the time he got to the punch line of his story he had lost the attention of most of his audience.

(prih TEN shus)	**pretentious**

pompous; making unjustified claims; outwardly extravagant

Picture this:
pretend shush

"*Pretend* we're not here—*shush*!"
The Smiths avoid *pretentious* people.

▪ I feel so *pretentious* wearing this $3,000 suit; I'm used to wearing a pair of jeans and a T-shirt all day.

▪ By nature reserved and modest, Jill has no interest in a *pretentious* wedding with hundreds of guests.

▪ We were amazed to see Bob, who has always been such a modest guy, acting in such a *pretentious* way; he's strutting down the street like he owns the whole town.

prodigal

wasteful; reckless
with money

Picture this:
prod a gull

Get off, gull, this
is my private
beach now.

TINY BEACH
SOLD
$0,000,000,000

A *prodigal* prince tries to *prod a gull*
to leave his private beach.

■ Some people regard the space program as a *prodigal*
display of America's wealth and technology.

■ The congressman criticized what he called the government's
prodigal spending and vowed to work for large cuts in
the budget.

■ The Hollywood actor's *prodigal* lifestyle left him in debt,
even though he was paid millions of dollars for every movie
that he starred in.

profusion

overabundance; excess

Picture this:
pro fusion

"A *profusion* of nuclear fusion plants!"
"Yeah, they're really *pro fusion* around here."

■ There has been a *profusion* of new car models this year.

■ There is such a *profusion* of food at this party that I can't possibly try all the dishes.

■ The *profusion* of life on Earth is so great that scientists have been able to study only a small fraction of it in depth.

proliferation *(pruh lif uh RAY shun)*

rapid growth; spread

Picture this:
pro lift her ration

Will the *pro lift her ration* since there's
been no fat *proliferation*?

■ Treaties between the United States and other countries have helped to limit the *proliferation* of nuclear weapons.

■ In the 1990s, there was a *proliferation* of cafés selling specialty coffees.

■ The *proliferation* of weeds on my front lawn leaves me with a decision to make: spend Sunday afternoon pulling weeds or ignore them and watch a football game on TV.

Memory Check 19

Match each word and its link to the corresponding definition.

penury	phenomena	ponderous
1. pen Yuri __	2. fin omen—ahhh! __	3. pond her Russ __
placate	proliferation	profusion
4. play Cate __	5. pro lift her ration __	6. pro fusion __
pithy	pretentious	perpetuate
7. pit he __	8. pretend shush __	9. purr pet you ate __
prodigal	peripheral	polemical
10. prod a gull __	11. pear for all __	12. polar Mick call __

a. pacify
b. rapid growth
c. wasteful
d. overabundance
e. pompous
f. observable facts

g. outer; marginal
h. concise; meaningful
i. aggressive in verbal attack
j. make something last
k. labored and dull
l. severe poverty

Showtime 19

Fill in the blanks in the following sentences with the word or set of words that best fits the meaning of the sentence as a whole.

1. "This family had better stop spending so much money," Mrs. Marks said, "or pretty soon we'll all be reduced to _____ ."
   a. phenomena   b. profusion   c. penury   d. proliferation   e. paucity

2. Critics _____ so much praise on Lucy's first novel that she began to think she was the next Jane Austen or Willa Cather.
   a. lavished   b. perpetuated   c. placated   d. incited   e. nurtured

3. It was announced that the senator's speech was going to be an objective assessment of the situation; instead, it turned out to be a (an) _____ attack on her opponents.
   a. polemical   b. prodigal   c. peripheral   d. pretentious   e. obstinate

4. Scientists are just beginning to explore the remarkable _____ of life that exists in the oceans of the world.

a. paucity   b. parody   c. nonchalance   d. profusion   e. oblivion

5. The _____ of flies this summer is one of the _____ that is being studied by scientists at the university.

a. profusion.....partisans
b. proliferation.....phenomena
c. penury.....phenomena
d. proliferation.....laments
e. paucity.....opportunists

6. The president of the company believes in _____ the talent of promising young employees by giving them assignments that are not merely _____ but are also vital to the company's success.

a. perpetuating.....polemical
b. mitigating.....pretentious
c. nurturing.....peripheral
d. placating.....peripheral
e. perpetuating.....pithy

7. After his death, the writer's family worked hard to _____ his memory in the mind of the public so that his works wouldn't fall into _____ .

a. perpetuate.....parody
b. lavish.....oblivion
c. nurture.....paucity
d. perpetuate.....oblivion
e. placate.....profusion

8. The after-dinner speaker is liked by audiences for her _____ comments about well-known people; they also appreciate the fact that she doesn't make long, _____ speeches.

a. pithy.....prodigal
b. peripheral.....munificent
c. pithy.....ponderous
d. ponderous.....polemical
e. mercenary.....pretentious

(pruh VIN shul)	provincial

limited in outlook;
unsophisticated

Picture this: **province shall**

UNIT 20

"This *province shall* remain *provincial*."

■ National newspapers generally avoid taking a *provincial* approach to reporting the news.

■ Coming from a big city, Bob found some of the attitudes of students from small towns at his university to be *provincial*.

■ Although she mixed well with the sophisticates in the city, at heart Holly was still a *provincial* small-town person.

quagmire

soft wet boggy land;
complex or dangerous
situation from which it is
difficult to free oneself

Picture this:
quack Myer

They chase *quack Myer* into a *quagmire*.

- The expedition faced a choice: Go the long way around the vast swamp and lose precious time or go through it and risk having their vehicles get stuck in a *quagmire*.

- The defense lawyer introduced so much evidence that the trial became bogged down in a *quagmire* of irrelevant information.

- Military leaders feel that involvement in a foreign country could lead the country into a *quagmire*.

querulous

complaining;
fretful

Picture this:
queer rule us

Johnny, you got only 99% on your assignment. That's *disgraceful*. I expect 100%.

Dad, why can't we go to *Spain* for vacation this year? We always do such *boring* things.

This chop is *undercooked*, *as usual*, Mildred.

HOME QUERULOUS HOME

Years ago our Grandpa gave a *queer rule* to *us*:
"Be *querulous*!"

- The *querulous* tourist spent most of his time in Europe complaining that Europe wasn't like home.

- Sophie must be naturally *querulous*; she's been complaining throughout our entire class trip to Washington, D.C.

- After six hours of nonstop driving, Ms. Chambers' six kids are becoming *querulous*.

quiescence

state of being at rest;
temporary inactivity

Picture this:
Qwee Essence

Qwee Essence brings *quiescence*.

■ The cease-fire brought a welcome period of *quiescence* in the long-running civil war.

■ Many astronomers believe that the universe will one day contract into a tiny point and reach *quiescence*.

■ The volcano is *quiescent* now, but when it erupts the village surrounding it will be destroyed.

ramble

wander aimlessly; talk
or write in a discursive,
aimless way

Picture this:
Ram Bull

Quite a fine day,
isn't it, Ram Bull?
Got time for
a coffee?

Ram Bull likes to *ramble* 'round town.

■ The biographer encouraged her subject to *ramble* on about
his childhood, hoping to discover details that would help
give an accurate picture of his early life.

■ The teacher's comment on Stan's essay was as follows:
"This long essay *rambles* too much. It needs to be better
organized. It can't wander aimlessly from topic to topic."

■ The governor's confused, *rambling* explanation did little
to help his critics understand why he vetoed the bill that he
had continually promised to support during the campaign.

rancor

bitterness;
hatred

Picture this:
rank core

That's **ridiculous**, Xircon! The data clearly establish that the core of this planet ranks high in **xylithium** in its **heaviest** state!

Nonsense, Xirla! You're wrong, as usual. The core definitely ranks highest in pure **xanthium!**

PLANET'S CORE

HEAVY METAL CORE SURVEY UNIT

They *rank* the *core* with *rancor*.

- There have been disagreements between the two people over the years, but never *rancor* or distrust.

- As a professional soldier, Colonel Gunn bore no personal *rancor* toward his foe; for him, the enemy was purely a force to be destroyed.

- The husband and wife agreed that they should get a divorce and that the process should be done without *rancor*.

(rant)	# rant

speak in an angry or
excited manner; rave

Picture this:
Ra ant

RAH RAH, Ra!
Oh great Ra!
Giver of Life!
RAH RAH, Ra!

"By *Ra*, that *ant* can *rant*!"

■ The principal *ranted* for an hour at the assembly about the
poor behavior of the students.

■ In London's Hyde Park, there's a place at which people
regularly make speeches *ranting* against the ills of the
world.

■ It's one thing to *rant* against social injustice; however, it's
quite another to actually do something to correct it.

rarefied

(RARE uh fied)

lofty; made
less dense

Picture this:
rare if I'd

"Back then it wasn't *rare if I'd* have
rarefied discussions with them."

■ Many world records were set in track and field at the
Mexico City Olympics in 1968 as a result of the *rarefied*
atmosphere.

■ The members of the mountain climbing expedition
experienced difficulty in breathing when they reached the
rarefied atmosphere near the top of the mountain.

■ The college freshman listened closely to the *rarefied*
discussion between the two distinguished philosophers,
but gave up trying to understand it after a while because it
was so abstract.

ratify

approve formally;
confirm; verify

Picture this:
rat if I

"I'll be a *rat if I ratify* this treaty."

■ The president's appointment of Judge Jones was *ratified* by the Senate after several days of debate.

■ The Constitutional amendment was approved by Congress; however, in order to become part of the Constitution it still must be *ratified* by three-quarters of the state legislatures.

■ The U.S. Senate *ratified* the treaty with Albania after a short debate.

raucous

(RAW kus)

harsh and shrill; disorderly
and boisterous

Picture this:
raw Cuz

A *raucous* cry—"The steaks are *raw, Cuz*!"

■ The inexperienced speaker had no idea how to quiet the *raucous* crowd so that she could begin her speech.

■ The *raucous* cries of the crows were becoming so annoying to the farmer that he wished he had a scarecrow.

■ The *raucous* crowd at the Super Bowl made it difficult for the players to hear their quarterback calling out signals.

(RAV uh nus)	ravenous

extremely hungry

Picture this:
raven us

Sir, Madam, we usually have three entrees to choose from, but the only choice today is *baked raven.*

"Then I guess it's baked *raven.*
Us folks are *ravenous*!"

■ After her one-week diet of nothing but vegetables, fruit, and rice, Kim was *ravenous.*

■ After receiving a taste of fame when she appeared on national television, the young actress became *ravenous* for even greater fame.

■ Please start the barbecue—I'm *ravenous.*

raze

(rayz)

destroy
completely

Picture this:
rays

Hot *rays raze* the city.

- The hotel was *razed* so that an office building could be built on the site.

- Returning after fifty years to the town he grew up in, Jim saw that the houses on his old street had been *razed* and a shopping center had been built on the site.

- Much of San Francisco was *razed* in the great fire of 1906.

Memory Check 20

Match each word and its link to the corresponding definition.

rarefied	rancor	querulous
1. **rare if I'd** __	2. **rank core** __	3. **queer rule us** __

provincial	quiescence	rant
4. **province shall** __	5. **Qwee Essence** __	6. **Ra ant** __

ramble	ratify	ravenous
7. **Ram Bull** __	8. **rat if I** __	9. **raven us** __

raucous	raze	quagmire
10. **raw Cuz** __	11. **rays** __	12. **quack Myer** __

a. speak excitedly
b. lofty
c. limited in outlook
d. wander aimlessly
e. harsh and shrill
f. complaining

g. temporary inactivity
h. destroy completely
i. boggy land
j. bitterness
k. approve formally
l. extremely hungry

Showtime 20

Fill in the blanks in the following sentences with the word or set of words that best fits the meaning of the sentence as a whole.

1. Critics sometimes accuse artists or writers who experiment with new styles of being _____ .
   a. raucous   b. provincial   c. querulous   d. ravenous   e. pretentious

2. The emperor made regular visits to _____ towns of his land so that he would know what was happening everywhere, not just in the big cities.
   a. rarefied   b. pretentious   c. querulous   d. provincial   e. ornate

3. The _____ between the union and the company is still strong even though the strike ended six months ago.
   a. rancor   b. phenomena   c. quagmire   d. rant   e. quiescence

4. Heavy rain turned the football field into such a (an) _____ that neither team could make much progress on offense.

a. profusion   b. proliferation   c. rancor   d. oblivion   e. quagmire

5. Still waiting for the meal to be served at 11:00 P.M., all the guests at the dinner party were becoming _____ , and some were becoming

_____ .

a. provincial.....querulous
b. polemical.....peripheral
c. ravenous.....querulous
d. quiescent.....raucous
e. ravenous.....rarefied

6. In his speech, the environmentalist _____ against the _____ use of Earth's natural resources.

a. ranted.....prodigal
b. rambled.....pretentious
c. razed.....prodigal
d. ratified.....raucous
e. ranted.....peripheral

7. After giving a long _____ speech, the senator finally came to his conclusion: The treaty should be _____ .

a. rarefied.....ranted
b. ravenous.....ratified
c. ponderous.....rarefied
d. rambling.....ratified
e. querulous.....razed

8. During the bitter dispute, there came a moment of _____ , and then the debate broke out again, more _____ than ever.

a. quiescence.....raucous
b. rancor.....rarefied
c. profusion.....raucous
d. opulence.....querulous
e. nonchalance.....partisan

recant

retract a previous statement; openly confess error

Picture this:
Rick can't

UNIT 21

Honest *Rick can't recant* his words.

■ After the witness *recanted* her testimony, the judge dismissed all charges against the accused.

■ Under pressure from her superiors, the government official *recanted* her statement criticizing her department's handling of the crisis.

■ The leader of the political party demanded that one of the members *recant* the position that she had expressed on the issue or be expelled from the party.

recount

(rih KOUNT)

narrate or tell;
count over again

Picture this:
Rick count

Recounting how *Rick* was picked to *count*
the votes in the *recount*.

■ Beth's grandfather loves to *recount* tales of his boyhood adventures.

■ The judge asked the witness to *recount* everything that had happened on the day that the crime was committed.

■ The autobiography *recounted* every important event in the senator's long and distinguished career.

rectify

set right; correct

Picture this:
wrecked if I

"I'll be *wrecked if I* don't *rectify*
my neighbor's behavior."

■ Please *rectify* this error in your calculation before submitting
the proposal to the boss.

■ The error in the newspaper article was *rectified* by a note in
the next day's edition apologizing for the mistake and giving
the correct information.

■ After a disappointing season with three wins and ten losses,
the football coach vowed to *rectify* whatever was wrong
with the team.

redundant

(rih DUN dunt)

unnecessary; repetitious; excessively wordy

Picture this:
redone dent

That's what the customer asked for—He told me to **"Redo the dent!"**

"Isn't a *redone dent* a little *redundant*?"

■ Legal terms such as "cease and desist" and "null and void" might appear *redundant* to the layperson.

■ Is the word "free" in the phrase "free gift" *redundant* since a gift is free by definition?

■ Engineers normally design spacecraft with *redundant* systems so that if the primary one fails the secondary one can take over.

relegate

banish to an inferior
position; delegate; assign

Picture this:
relic eight

There hasn't been much interest
in **Relic Eight** lately. Put it
in the rear display.

They *relegate relic eight* to the rear.

■ Although she skated almost perfectly in the freestyle portion
of the competition, Susie's weak performance in the earlier
part of the competition *relegated* her to fifth place in the
overall standings.

■ After years of dedicated service to her country, the retired
senator found it difficult being *relegated* to the position
of advisor.

■ The newly elected congressman was *relegated* to the lowest
position on the House committee.

remorse

guilt;
bitter regret

Picture this:
rim horse

A *rim horse* feeling *remorse.*

■ Many people find it easier to forgive someone for doing something wrong if the person shows *remorse.*

■ Jim felt *remorse* for the rest of his life as a result of one moment of stupidity in his youth when he drove his car recklessly and hit a child on a bicycle, causing serious injury to the child.

■ The soldier told himself that he was only doing his duty when he was sent to war and so he shouldn't feel guilty; however, he still felt some *remorse.*

repel

drive away;
disgust

Picture this:
reap hell

"*Repel* the Goths or *reap hell!*"

■ Joan's arrogant manner, rather than *repelling* men, as one would suspect, seems to attract them.

■ The first duty of the military is to *repel* an enemy invasion.

■ The manufacturer claims that this ointment *repels* mosquitoes, but all it does for me is make my skin oily; the mosquitoes are biting me just as much as ever.

reprehensible

deserving
blame

Picture this:
rep pre-hens Sibyl

The *rep* for *pre-hens*, *Sibyl*,
denounces *reprehensible* behavior.

■ The president condemned the terrorist attack as a cowardly,
reprehensible act.

■ The United Nations Security Council unanimously
condemned as *reprehensible* the country's threat to
invade its neighbor.

■ Human beings seem to be capable of, at one extreme,
completely *reprehensible* acts and, at the other extreme,
the most incredible acts of kindness and self-sacrifice.

(rih PYOO dee ayt)	repudiate

reject strongly as wrong;
reject the validity or
authority of

Picture this:
rep you'd date

Bill Reese—he's the kind of *rep you'd date*—
he *repudiates* gross behavior.

■ After his deep religious experience, James *repudiated* his
past life of pleasure-seeking and dedicated himself to
working to help others.

■ The politician *repudiated* the accusation against him of
making illegal use of government funds.

■ Even under torture, the priest refused to *repudiate* his
beliefs.

rescind

cancel

Picture this:
Reese sent

Reese sent his team a memo to
rescind his previous one.

MEMO FROM MR. REESE:

Regarding that earlier
memo about everybody
being expected to work
on Christmas day....

Just kidding.

■ The state supreme court *rescinded* the results of the election
as a result of major irregularities in the vote counting.

■ The president of the company told his counterpart in the
other firm that his offer to buy out its electronics division
would be *rescinded* if not accepted by Friday at 5:00 P.M.

■ The movement to *rescind* the new taxes quickly gained
momentum after most politicians came out in support of it.

reserve

self-restraint in expression

TO THE HONORABLE MR. REESE:

I am writing to express some degree of interest in you and I attending the company Christmas party on the 24th. Please notify me within 2 days if you would serve as my date.
Respectfully, Ms Jones

With *reserve*, she asks Mr. *Reese* to *serve*
as her date for the Christmas party.

■ William has an air of *reserve* that even his best friends seldom try to break through.

■ The rock singer has a *reserve* that many of his fans find appealing.

■ Unlike many movie stars, who are often outgoing and talkative, Ms. Starlet is shy and *reserved*.

resigned

(rih ZINED)

accepting one's fate;
unresisting

Picture this:
Reese signed

Resigned to his fate, *Reese signed* in late.

■ Having no qualifications beyond a sixth-grade education, John was *resigned* to a lifetime of dull, menial jobs.

■ Having just turned 97, Mr. James knew that he had lived a long life and was *resigned* to the fact that it would end soon.

■ The veteran astronaut is *resigned* to the fact that he will be too old to be part of an expedition to Mars.

Memory Check 21

Match each word and its link to the corresponding definition.

recant   repel   repudiate

1. **Rick can't** __   2. **reap hell** __   3. **rep you'd date** __

relegate   reprehensible   rectify

4. **relic eight** __   5. **rep pre-hens Sibyl** __ 6. **wrecked if I** __

rescind   redundant   resigned

7. **Reese sent** __   8. **redone dent** __   9. **Reese signed** __

recount   remorse   reserve

10. **Rick count** __   11. **rim horse** __   12. **Reese serve** __

a. drive away
b. correct
c. deserving blame
d. cancel
e. accepting one's fate
f. unnecessary

g. narrate
h. guilt
i. self-restraint in expression
j. retract a previous statement
k. banish to an inferior position
l. reject strongly as wrong

Showtime 21

Fill in the blanks in the following sentences with the word or set of words that best fits the meaning of the sentence as a whole.

1. The _____ atmosphere at which modern jet liners cruise makes it necessary that the passenger cabin be pressurized.

   a. rarefied b. quiescent c. reprehensible d. redundant e. reserved

2. The _____ crowd became so unruly that the police had to be called in to restore order.

   a. resigned b. raucous c. ravenous d. redundant e. reserved

3. Surrounded by enemy forces and outgunned, the lieutenant _____ himself to the fact that he would have to surrender or see his men killed.

   a. rambled b. resigned c. recounted d. relegated e. ratified

4. The college _____ its scholarship offer to Ted after he admitted to cheating on his final exam in high school.

    a. recanted   b. recounted   c. rescinded   d. relegated   e. repudiated

5. In the book _____ the history of our town, my grandfather, who was its main founder, is _____ to a secondary role.

    a. recanting.....repelled
    b. recounting.....relegated
    c. rectifying.....repelled
    d. rescinding.....rectified
    e. repelling.....relegated

6. The soldier felt no _____ for killing enemy soldiers in the process of _____ the invading army.

    a. reserve.....repudiating
    b. rancor.....repelling
    c. remorse.....repelling
    d. quiescence.....recanting
    e. reserve....recounting

7. Unable to _____ the problem with their main computer, the astronauts switched to a _____ system that allowed them to continue their mission.

    a. rectify.....redundant
    b. repel.....rarefied
    c. recount.....resigned
    d. relegate.....reprehensible
    e. repudiate.....redundant

8. The general _____ the reporter's suggestion that his forces had _____ the civilian area of the enemy's city intentionally and vowed that those responsible would be brought to justice.

    a. repelled.....recanted
    b. rescinded.....ranted
    c. repudiated.....razed
    d. recanted.....repelled
    e. rectified.....razed

restraint

moderation or self-control;
controlling force; restriction

Picture this:
Reese trained

UNIT 22

Sorry, we can't have a date this week. I'm in training.

When *Reese trained* for the company race,
he used *restraint* in dating.

■ The famous writer exercised *restraint* when the critic told
him to his face that his latest book was the worst book he
had ever read; he simply walked away.

■ The judge ordered the police to use *restraint* in taking the
elderly demonstrators into custody.

■ The dictator showed no *restraint* in squashing the rebellion;
she ordered anyone who had participated to be executed.

reticence

uncommunicativeness; reserve; inclination to silence

Picture this:
Rhet a sense

I don't really *need* a reading.

She feels from *Rhet a sense* of *reticence*.

■ Because she was concerned about his extreme *reticence* in class, Samuel's fourth-grade teacher called his parents to ask them if he was also uncommunicative at home.

■ It was no time for *reticence*; someone had to speak out against the injustice.

■ A career in the CIA had made Frank *reticent* about discussing anything even remotely connected to national security.

retract

withdraw;
take back

Picture this:
Rhet tracked

I must **take back** what I said
to the gypsy—I **do** need a fortune teller.

Rhet tracked through the woods
to *retract* his words.

■ The two companies agreed to *retract* damaging comments
that each had made about the products of the other.

■ In the heat of the campaign debate, the candidate made
accusations against her opponent that she later *retracted*
and apologized for.

■ The inventor *retracted* her claim that she had invented the
new device completely on her own.

rhetorical

pertaining to effective
communication; insincere
in language; characterized
by overly elaborate,
pompous language

Picture this:
Rhet oracle

What is the meaning of life?... I'm glad you asked
me that...In my great wisdom, I have delved into this
complicated matter and reached a conclusion...
... that *may* be correct under *certain* conditions.
However, it must be borne in mind
that there are *many* *factors* to
consider, and so we would ask
you to keep in mind the
distinct possibility of error,
and, if not error, at least
a degree of uncertainty which o...

THE ORACLE
IS IN

Rhet questions the *oracle* and
receives a *rhetorical* response.

- This line from the Bible uses the *rhetorical* device of
  repetition of the same word: "Vanity of vanities, saith the
  Preacher, vanity of vanities; all is vanity."

- *Rhetorical* techniques can be used to make your writing
  more effective.

- The speech consisted mainly of empty *rhetoric* rather than
  meaningful ideas.

rigor

severity;
strictness

Picture this:
rig Gore

Make fast the rigging, me hearties!

GORE

The *rig* is checked by Captain *Gore* with *rigor*.

■ In the early years of ocean exploration, many people did not survive the *rigors* of long voyages on the sea.

■ Hal's French teacher suggested that he apply the same *rigor* he brought to memorizing football statistics to memorizing conjugations of irregular French verbs.

■ Modern science has brought a new *rigor* to the study of nature.

robust

vigorous;
strong

Picture this:
row bust

*"**Row**, **row**, **row** your **bust** gently down the stream,"*
sings the *robust* rower.

■ The general warned the enemy commander that any attack
would be met immediately with a *robust* counterattack.

■ A heavyweight boxer must be *robust* enough to withstand
the extremely hard punches of his opponents.

■ Before the United States entered World War II, the
American Army General George Patton said that America
would win the war because its soldiers were more *robust*
than those of the enemy.

sage

person celebrated for wisdom

Picture this:
sage

This *sage* swears by *sage*.

- Although she didn't consider herself a *sage*, Janice's friends always sought her advice when they encountered a problem in their lives.

- The teachings of the ancient Chinese *sage* Confucius are still greatly respected today.

- I was surprised to hear such *sage* words from such a young person.

sanction

approve;
ratify

Picture this:
sank shun

"I cannot *sanction* this route.
It's where scores of ships *sank*. *Shun* it!"

■ The World Cup soccer tournament is *sanctioned* by the sport's governing body, FIFA.

■ The governor *sanctioned* the plan to make the administration of the criminal justice system more efficient.

■ "Pirate" short-wave stations operating without government *sanction* filled the airwaves during the Cold War.

satirical

mocking; characterized by sarcastic wit to attack or expose folly

Picture this:
satyr Rick calls

Satyr Rick calls the Park people
to make a *satirical* comment!

- Although the students did not intend for their *satirical* skit to be insulting to anyone, most of the audience thought it was tasteless and offensive.

- *Satirical* writing generally makes fun of a fault in society or in human nature, often with the intention of bringing such faults to people's attention.

- Television programs such as *Saturday Night Live* feature *satirical* comedy that pokes fun at modern society.

saturate

(SATCH uh rayt)

soak
thoroughly

Picture this:
sat shore ate

On Saturdays they *sat* on the *shore* and
ate fries that they'd *saturated* in ketchup.

■ The heavy rain before the football game *saturated* the turf,
making it difficult for players to execute plays properly.

■ I left the sprinkler on overnight by mistake; now the ground
is so *saturated* that I can't lie on a blanket on the grass to
catch some rays.

■ It's so humid that when I go jogging my shirt becomes
saturated with sweat very quickly.

tasty; pleasing, attractive, or agreeable

Picture this:
save Orry

Orry loves savory stuff. Save the apple pie and other desserts for him.

"*Save Orry* all the *savory* stuff."

■ A table full of *savory* snacks! There goes my diet!

■ The big time gangster hired an advertising consultant to help give the mob a more *savory* public image.

■ There were so many *savory* desserts at the buffet that Wayne had trouble choosing which one to try first.

scanty

meager;
insufficient

Picture this:
scan tea

Tea Police *scan* the *tea* party for *scanty* outfits.

■ With supplies becoming *scanty*, the commander decided to halt the advance and concentrate on obtaining food, water, and other necessities.

■ The country's *scanty* reserves of oil make it dependent on importing oil from other countries.

■ The content of Barbara's history essay was so *scanty* that she received a D on it.

324

Memory Check 22

Match each word and its link to the corresponding definition.

restraint	robust	rhetorical
1. **Reese trained** __	2. **row bust** __	3. **Rhet oracle** __

rigor	reticence	sanction
4. **rig Gore** __	5. **Rhet a sense** __	6. **sank shun** __

retract	saturate	scanty
7. **Rhet tracked** __	8. **sat shore ate** __	9. **scan tea** __

satirical	sage	savory
10. **satyr Rick calls** __	11. **sage** __	12. **save Orry** __

a. insincere in language
b. inclination to silence
c. strong
d. soak thoroughly
e. meager
f. approve

g. take back
h. a wise person
i. self-control
j. strictness
k. tasty; pleasing
l. mocking

Showtime 22

Fill in the blanks in the following sentences with the word or set of words that best fits the meaning of the sentence as a whole.

1. The astronomer _____ his claim that he had discovered a new planet in the solar system after he realized that he had made an error in his observation.
   a. recounted b. rectified c. sanctioned d. retracted e. ratified

2. The witness _____ the confession that he had made to the police after his arrest, saying that he had been upset when he made it.
   a. sanctioned b. relegated c. ratified d. repelled e. recanted

3. The student found that behind her teacher's _____ was a highly emotional man.
   a. reserve b. opulence c. rigor d. remorse e. rancor

4. The bikini is a _____ bathing suit named after a coral reef in the Pacific Ocean where an atom bomb was tested in 1946.

    a. rhetorical   b. scanty   c. satirical   d. robust   e. redundant

5. The doctor suggested to her patient that he should exercise _____ and avoid his favorite _____ foods in order to lose weight.

    a. reticence.....saturated
    b. quiescence.....scanty
    c. restraint.....savory
    d. rigor.....savory
    e. remorse.....reprehensible

6. The _____ expressed his views with _____ because he believed that truth is something difficult for even a wise person to express and convey to others.

    a. pacifist.....reserve
    b. opportunist.....restraint
    c. orator.....rigor
    d. partisan.....remorse
    e. sage.....reticence

7. The king found the _____ skit about his rule _____ and ordered everyone involved with it to be jailed.

    a. satirical.....reprehensible
    b. rhetorical....reprehensible
    c. robust.....provincial
    d. satirical.....savory
    e. rhetorical.....redundant

8. The United Nations Security Council _____ a _____ military action by the major powers to prevent the small country from being conquered by its large, aggressive neighbor.

    a. sanctioned.....robust
    b. saturated.....raucous
    c. retracted.....scanty
    d. ratified.....redundant
    e. ratified.....scanty

scrupulous

conscientious;
extremely thorough

Picture this:
screw pull us

UNIT 23

"Can this *screw pull us* through?
We must make a *scrupulous* check!"

■ Ralph's *scrupulous* preparation for the English test resulted in his receiving a grade of A.

■ The groundskeeper at the baseball stadium is *scrupulous* about maintaining the infield grass but doesn't bother much with the outfield grass.

■ Coach Ford's preparation of our team for the championship game against State was *scrupulous*; he made sure that every detail was perfectly planned.

scrutinize (SKROOT uh nyze)

examine closely
and critically

Picture this:
screw tin eyes

Trainees *screw tin eyes* on the doors while
the boss *scrutinizes* their technique.

■ Mandy *scrutinized* her sister's appearance and then said,
"I pronounce you ready to go to the dance. You look great."

■ During the interrogation the detective *scrutinized* the
suspect's face for an indication that he was not telling
the truth about his involvement in the crime.

■ The computer programmer *scrutinized* the program that
she had written to see if there were any errors in it.

(sih KLOO zhun)

seclusion

isolation;
solitude

Picture this:
sick illusion

They say that the old hermit who lives there believes he's the last human on earth.

What a sick illusion.

LIMA

He lives in *seclusion* with his *sick illusion*.

■ The hermit lives in *seclusion* in a cabin in the mountains.

■ Some writers can do their work with others around, but others prefer quiet and *seclusion.*

■ The Hollywood actor went into *seclusion* soon after the news media reported the scandal.

servile

slavish;
submissive

Picture this:
serve vial

Sir Vile tells his *servile* slave to *serve*
the *vial* of poison to his guest.

■ People who are used to being nice are sometimes so *servile*
that they are unable to say "No" to an unreasonable request.

■ After half the workers in the plant had been laid off, Sally
noticed that some employees were becoming *servile* in their
relationship with the plant manager.

■ Servants in Victorian England were generally expected to be
servile toward their employers.

(SLUG ish)	sluggish

slow; lazy;
lacking energy

Picture this:
slug

A *sluggish slug* pulls Bee's luggage.

■ The first three laps of the 5,000-meter event were run at a *sluggish* pace, but on the fourth lap the state champion suddenly picked up the pace.

■ Because economic growth has been *sluggish*, Congress voted to reduce taxes to try to stimulate spending.

■ My car was *sluggish* until I cleaned the carburetor; now it accelerates like a car in a drag race.

somber

(SOM bur)

gloomy; depressing;
dark; drab

Picture this:
some brrr

"That's *some brrr* you have there,"
he says to the *somber* bird.

■ The *somber* mood in the room when I returned told me that something terrible had happened.

■ The atmosphere was *somber* in party headquarters as news of the landslide defeat came in.

■ The president looked *somber* as he announced that war had broken out between our nation and another nation.

soporific

sleep-causing;
marked by sleepiness

Picture this:
Soap Horrific

He used to fall asleep in the bath until he tried *"Soap Horrific."*

Soap Horrific. Soap that's not *soporific*.

■ Terri finds nothing more *soporific* than listening to classical music; she's usually asleep before the end of the first movement of a symphony.

■ If you have trouble getting to sleep, try reading a long, boring, *soporific* book.

■ A lot of guys find romantic comedies *soporific* because there's too much talk and not enough action.

sporadic

occurring
irregularly

Picture this:
spore addict

The *spore addict* waits for *sporadic* spores.

■ The advancing army met *sporadic* enemy resistance, but it used heavy artillery barrages to destroy these few units that were still putting up a fight.

■ Although there have only been *sporadic* outbreaks of the flu this winter, government health officials are monitoring the situation carefully.

■ The military announced that they had taken complete control of the enemy city; however, *sporadic* gunfire could still be heard in some areas.

stagnant

motionless;
stale; dull

Picture this:
Stag 'n' Ant

Stagnant business at the ***Stag 'n' Ant***.

■ During the long drought all that was left of Lake Weir was
stagnant water one foot deep.

■ The government reported that economic growth had been
stagnant during the last quarter of the year and that
measures were therefore being considered to stimulate
the economy.

■ Fewer people have been investing in the stock market
recently because it's been *stagnant* the last few months.

stolid

showing little emotion

Picture this:
stole lid

Although someone *stole* the *lid*,
the chef remains *stolid*.

■ Awaiting sentencing, the convicted man could get no hint of his fate from the *stolid* expression on the judge's face.

■ Behind the banker's *stolid*, conservative appearance is a man whose hobby is parachuting from airplanes and who uses weekends for nonstop partying.

■ The commander, remaining *stolid* despite the heavy causalities his unit had suffered in the assault, ordered a fresh attack.

(STRIDE nt)	strident

loud and harsh;
insistent

Picture this:
S.S. Trident

The **S.S. Trident** lets out a **strident** wail.

■ Demands by shareholders for the removal of the chairman of the company from his position became more *strident* after it was learned that he had covered up the company's large losses.

■ Despite *strident* protests from environmentalists, the plan to build a dam in the conservation area was approved by the government.

■ Calls from the alumni for the head football coach to resign grew more *strident* after the team finished with a record of two wins and eleven losses.

337

stupefied

made numb;
stunned; amazed

Picture this:
stoop if I'd

"I'd always sit on the *stoop if I'd* been *stupefied* by a wild ride with the guys from McBride."

■ After a barrage of punches had left the boxer *stupefied*, the referee stepped in and stopped the fight.

■ The soldiers were *stupefied* by the ferocious artillery barrage their unit came under.

■ We stood *stupefied*, watching the gigantic UFO descend.

Memory Check 23

Match each word and its link to the corresponding definition.

sporadic | somber | seclusion
1. spore addict __ | **2. some brrr** __ | **3. sick illusion** __

servile | stolid | stupefied
4. serve vial __ | **5. stole lid** __ | **6. stoop if I'd** __

soporific | scrutinize | strident
7. Soap Horrific __ | **8. screw tin eyes** __ | **9. S.S. Trident** __

stagnant | scrupulous | sluggish
10. Stag 'n' Ant __ | **11. screw pull us** __ | **12. slug** __

a. motionless
b. examine closely
c. stunned
d. solitude
e. gloomy
f. slavish

g. sleep-causing
h. occurring irregularly
i. slow
j. loud and harsh
k. extremely thorough
l. showing little emotion

Showtime 23

Fill in the blanks in the following sentences with the word or set of words that best fits the meaning of the sentence as a whole.

1. Tammy says that most of the books she uses to prepare for the SAT are so _____ that she can't stay awake for long enough to learn much from them.

   a. scrupulous   b. sporadic   c. stupefied   d. strident   e. soporific

2. Although Tammy's parents are worried because their daughter will receive her SAT results very soon, they remain _____ , trying to control their feelings.

   a. scrupulous   b. stolid   c. somber   d. servile   e. sluggish

3. Tammy's parents didn't expect her to be _____ in following their instructions to prepare thoroughly for the SAT, but they did expect her to make a reasonably good effort.

   a. somber   b. scrupulous   c. soporific   d. sporadic   e. strident

4. Tammy had a _____ look on her face after she spent an entire weekend trying to memorize all the words on the word list.

    a. strident   b. stagnant   c. stupefied   d. sporadic   e. scrupulous

5. Tammy's parents thought it unlikely that she had studied the SAT preparation books they had bought for her _____ ; they had seen her make a _____ effort to study but were worried that this preparation wouldn't be enough to help her get a good score.

    a. somberly.....strident
    b. sluggishly.....scrupulous
    c. stolidly.....sluggish
    d. scrupulously.....sporadic
    e. satirically.....sporadic

6. Tammy says that SAT reading questions dealing with _____ techniques are the most difficult because intellectual _____ is required to answer them correctly.

    a. satirical.....reticence
    b. rhetorical.....rigor
    c. stolid.....seclusion
    d. redundant.....profusion
    e. satirical.....quiescence

7. After Tammy received her SAT results, she went into her room to _____ them in _____ .

    a. scrutinize.....seclusion
    b. sanction.....saturate
    c. retract.....seclusion
    d. rectify.....reticence
    e. scrutinize.....profusion

8. Tammy's parents were _____ as they waited for her to tell them how she had done on the SAT; although they had been _____ in their insistence that she study hard for the test, they were afraid that she had not done enough preparation.

    a. somber.....strident
    b. servile.....sporadic
    c. sluggish.....scrupulous
    d. stolid.....stagnant
    e. stupefied.....raucous

subside

settle down; descend;
grow quiet

Picture this:
sub side

UNIT 24

The *sub* lay on its *side* waiting
for the attack to *subside*.

■ After the argument, Jean's anger *subsided*, and she
apologized to her friend for having been rude.

■ The excitement in our school about winning the state
football championship has finally *subsided* three months
after the victory.

■ After the floodwaters *subsided*, the farmer surveyed the
damage the flood had caused to his crops.

(soo pur FISH ul)

concerned only with
the obvious; shallow;
near the surface

Picture this:
super facial

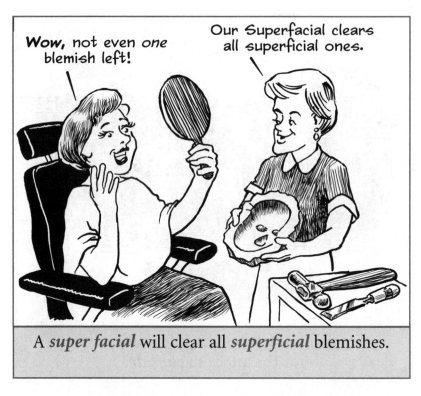

Wow, not even one blemish left!

Our Superfacial clears all superficial ones.

A *super facial* will clear all *superficial* blemishes.

- Because his injury was only *superficial*, our quarterback was able to return to the game after receiving some treatment.

- My English teacher expects us to analyze in depth the poems we studied; he gives little credit for a *superficial* analysis.

- Only very talented novelists have the ability to give readers more than a *superficial* picture of the characters in their books.

superfluous

unnecessary; excessive; overabundant

Picture this:
Super Flu us

"The *Super Flu* left *us* with *superfluous* tissues."

■ When writing your answer on a test, you should avoid *superfluous* comments and just stick to the important points.

■ This film has already received hundreds of glowing reviews; any more would be *superfluous.*

■ This dessert is made of chocolate ice cream, chocolate mousse, chocolate fudge, and chocolate chips; would some chocolate syrup be *superfluous*?

surfeit

(SUR fit)

noun: excess; overindulgence

verb: indulge to excess in anything

Picture this:
Surf It

At Waikiki's *Surf It*, a *surfeit* of Surf 'n' Turf.

■ There has been a *surfeit* of movies this year with a female superhero in the leading role.

■ Between Christmas Day and New Year's Day every year, television viewers are *surfeited* with college football games.

■ Tom's appetite for computer games was *surfeited* after he played them practically nonstop over the summer vacation.

surreptitious

done in a secret
way; hidden

Picture this:
Sir Repetitious

I must be *surreptitious.*
I must be *surreptitious.*
I must be *surreptitious.*
I must be *surreptitious.*
I must be *surreptitious.*
I must be *surreptitious.*

Sir Repetitious in a *surreptitious* operation.

■ We have to be *surreptitious* in preparing Dad's surprise party so he doesn't become suspicious of what we're doing.

■ The movie star made a *surreptitious* exit through the back door of the studio to avoid reporters.

■ The intelligence officer *surreptitiously* monitored the enemy naval operation from his hidden observation post.

sycophant

(SIK uh funt)

self-seeker who tries to gain favor by flattering important people; bootlicker

Picture this:
sick of aunt

I think you're the most handsome, bravest and smartest prince in history. Of course you *still* need my advice, so I want you to raise my spending money to one million a year...

Sick of his *aunt*—a slick *sycophant*— he booted her out of his castle.

■ Val is a shameless *sycophant*; she is constantly telling her boss that his ideas are the best ideas that anyone has ever had and that he should be the president of the company.

■ Hoping to get the best mark in the class, the *sycophant* flattered his teacher at every opportunity.

■ Fed up with all the *sycophants* around him always agreeing with everything he said, the CEO screamed at them, "Stop saying 'Yes' to everything I say!" "Yes," they all replied in unison.

tantamount

equivalent in
effect or value

Picture this:
Tant a mount

PRETTY CLOSE TO K2 IN HEIGHT

UNFAIR TO ALPACAS

ALPACA RIGHTS

CLIMBING EL PICO IS TOO MUCH FOR ALPACAS

TANT

Using *Tant* as *a mount* to ascend El Pico in Peru is
tantamount to saying alpacas' rights are few!

■ In Mr. Rogers' math class, any remark that suggests the
slightest bit of disrespect for the wonders of mathematics is
regarded as *tantamount* to saying that studying the subject
is a waste of time.

■ The political party that Mr. Stevens belongs to is so
dominant in this county that winning the nomination for
an office is *tantamount* to winning the office itself.

■ The harsh threat that the government made to the leaders of
the neighboring country is *tantamount* to a declaration
of war.

tenacity

(tuh NAS ih tee)

firmness;
persistence

Picture this:
ten a city

With great *tenacity*, the spacecraft
continue their attack, *ten* to *a city*.

■ If you have enough *tenacity*, you can learn all 315 vocabulary words in this book.

■ Carol demonstrated remarkable *tenacity* in achieving her goal of receiving a perfect score on the SAT; she studied for an hour every day for a year, never allowing herself to be distracted.

■ Thomas Edison showed incredible *tenacity* in his invention of the light bulb; he tried thousands of substances in the filament before finding one that worked properly.

terrestrial

related to the earth;
pertaining to the land

Picture this:
Terrace tree all

To the *Terrace tree*, *all terrestrials*
are taken for tasting.

■ Astronomers using *terrestrial* optical telescopes to observe
the heavens often complain that light from man-made
sources is making it increasingly difficult for them to see
very faint objects clearly.

■ *Terrestrial* tracking stations around the world observe the
course of probes sent from Earth to explore the solar system.

■ Some people believe that money spent on the space program
should instead be spent to solve *terrestrial* problems.

threadbare

(THRED bare)

worn through till
the threads show;
shabby and poor

Picture this:
Thread Bear

Thread Bear takes orders
from ***threadbare*** customers.

■ Jack's wife tells him that wearing *threadbare* suits to work
makes him look poor; Jack's reply is, "I will be poor if I have
to keep buying new suits."

■ Since my favorite sweater has become *threadbare*, I'll have
to buy a new one.

■ Amber is really good at sewing; she took a *threadbare*
dress she got in the secondhand store and made it look
practically new.

tirade

extended scolding;
long angry speech
denouncing something

Picture this:
tie raid

Why on earth did you sneak in here and steal a tie? It's *unbelievable.* Mark my words, young man, **you will be punished for this!** These ties are like *gold* to me. I can't believe . . .
. . . .
. . . . . .
. . .

A *tirade* at the *tie raid*.

■ Fed up with his wife's spending on clothes, Mr. Banks began a *tirade* against modern fashion and the stupidity of people conforming to it.

■ The magazine editorial is basically a *tirade* by the retiring publisher against the declining quality of reporting in newspapers and magazines.

■ After Simon failed French, his father launched into a *tirade* about how he had a son who was too lazy to study and would never succeed like his father had.

torpor
(TOR per)

physical or mental inactivity; sluggishness; dormancy

Picture this:
tour pour

During the *tour* when it started to *pour*,
they fell into a deep *torpor*.

■ In the spring, the snake began to recover from its winter *torpor* and went in search of a good breakfast.

■ My physics teacher asked the class to shake itself out of its mental *torpor* and really *think* about the problem.

■ The hot, humid weather has induced in everyone a *torpor* that makes it difficult to do much of anything at all.

Memory Check 24

Match each word and its link to the corresponding definition.

sycophant	superfluous	threadbare
1. sick of aunt __	2. Super Flu us __	3. Thread Bear __
tantamount	subside	tenacity
4. Tant a mount __	5. sub side __	6. ten a city __
surfeit	surreptitious	tirade
7. Surf It __	8. Sir Repetitious __	9. tie raid __
terrestrial	superficial	torpor
10. Terrace tree all __	11. super facial __	12. tour pour __

a. sluggishness
b. shallow
c. indulge to excess in anything
d. bootlicker
e. settle down
f. extended scolding

g. equivalent in effect of value
h. worn through
i. related to the earth
j. unnecessary
k. persistence
l. done in a secret way

Showtime 24

Fill in the blanks in the following sentences with the word or set of words that best fits the meaning of the sentence as a whole.

1. When you go camping, don't drink water from _____ streams because there could be harmful bacteria or other organisms in them.
   a. superficial   b. threadbare   c. stagnant
   d. terrestrial   e. superfluous

2. When writing your college admissions essays, avoid including _____ words that don't add anything to your story and message.
   a. surreptitious   b. superfluous   c. threadbare
   d. strident   e. tantamount

3. Jim's date for the formal was horrified when he showed up at her house wearing a _____ suit that looked like it had been handed down to him by his grandfather.
   a. superficial   b. servile   c. superfluous   d. threadbare   e. savory

4. In the spring, hibernating bears come out of their winter _____ and start hunting for food.

    a. tenacity   b. surfeit   c. torpor   d. tirade   e. reticence

5. The class _____ is well-known for doing anything he can to butter up teachers; he doesn't even bother to flatter them _____ .

    a. sycophant.....superfluously
    b. terrestrial.....superficially
    c. sage.....sporadically
    d. rancor.....surreptitiously
    e. sycophant.....surreptitiously

6. Tammy's mother bought a _____ of SAT preparation books for her daughter, most of which now sit in a big pile on the floor, unused because Tammy thinks their explanations are too _____ to be of much help.

    a. surfeit.....superficial
    b. torpor.....threadbare
    c. seclusion.....superfluous
    d. quagmire.....superficial
    e. tirade.....tantamount

7. After Tammy admitted that she hadn't studied her SAT prep books for two weeks, her father launched into a _____ , saying that she had better start studying or he wouldn't help pay for her to go to college; Tammy waited, hoping that her father's anger would _____ .

    a. sycophant.....subside
    b. surfeit.....scrutinize
    c. tirade.....subside
    d. torpor.....retract
    e. sage.....relegate

8. Dave's progress in preparing for the SAT has been _____ because he lacks the _____ to stick to a regular plan of study.

    a. sporadic.....tenacity
    b. superficial.....seclusion
    c. superfluous.....tenacity
    d. surreptitious.....reticence
    e. subside.....tenacity

trivial;
unimportant

Picture this:
Try Fling

UNIT 25

Try Fling is too *trifling* for the Frisbee Champ.

■ The poet was unconcerned with what he considered the
trifling fact that his readership consisted of only his wife,
her brother, and three friends.

■ One thousand dollars may be a *trifling* sum to a millionaire,
but to a poor family it's enough money to buy a lot of
necessities such as food and clothing.

■ Beth refused her friend's offer to pay back the $3 she had
borrowed for parking, saying it was just a *trifling* amount
of money.

truncate

(TRUNG kayt)

shorten; cut
the top off

Picture this:
trunk Kate

The tree they did *truncate*—
so, by the *trunk Kate* wept.

■ When his English teacher handed out the 1,000-page novel for the class to start reading, Larry piped up, "Can't we read the *truncated* version instead?"

■ My pleasant conversation with an old friend was *truncated* by an important telephone call.

■ Network television officials decided to *truncate* the broadcast of the football game because it had gone on way past the time scheduled for it and would interfere with the broadcast of a feature movie.

turmoil

great commotion and confusion

Picture this:
term oil

He burns the *term oil*, ignoring the *turmoil* outside.

■ Adolescence is often regarded as a time of emotional *turmoil*.

■ There was *turmoil* in the political party after its most influential and respected member announced that he was quitting the party and joining the opposing party.

■ *Turmoil* ensued when everyone exited the rock concert at once.

undermine

weaken; sap

Picture this:
under mine

"They put the cockroach *under mine*
to *undermine* my entry!"

■ Rod's efforts to improve his vocabulary were *undermined*
by his refusal to reinforce his learning by reading some good
books and magazines.

■ It's very important that a teacher's authority over his or her
class not be *undermined*.

■ The prosecutor's case was *undermined* when the star
witness admitted that she may have been mistaken in her
identification of the accused.

uniformity

sameness

Picture this:
uniform at tea

ANNUAL SCHOOL TEA

They wear the *uniform at tea*
to promote *uniformity*.

■ The pollster found a great *uniformity* of views on the central issues confronting the nation; on less important issues, however, there was a great diversity of views.

■ The editor of the encyclopedia tries to maintain a *uniformity* of style from article to article so that the reader will be able to focus on the information itself rather than on how it's presented.

■ The company doesn't expect *uniformity* in dress, but it does expect employees to dress appropriately and not wear outlandish outfits.

unwarranted

unjustified; groundless;
undeserved

Picture this:
a warrant Ted

"*A warrant*?" *Ted* asked. "That's *unwarranted*."

- In seeking answers to questions about nature, a scientist must be careful not to make ***unwarranted*** assumptions.

- Jason was apologetic after it turned out that his accusation was ***unwarranted***.

- The assumption that any tall person can be a good basketball player is ***unwarranted***.

(VAY puh rise)	vaporize

turn into
vapor

Picture this:
vapor eyes

The girl with *vapor eyes* will *vaporize* you!

■ Military planners are working on a space-based weapon that would be able to *vaporize* entire cities with a burst of high energy.

■ After taking measurements of the sun's high-energy radiation, the space probe plunged toward the sun's surface and was *vaporized*.

■ At the end of the science fiction movie, the hero fired a gigantic ray gun at the hostile aliens, *vaporizing* them.

viable

(VI uh bul)

practical or workable;
capable of maintaining life

Picture this:
Vye a bull

Come on and ride one, Vye!

I'm afraid I can't.

It's just not *viable*. *Vye* is not able to ride *a bull*.

- Education experts recommended that the school reduce the average class size from thirty to twenty, but the school board said it was not economically *viable*.

- Engineers are working to create a *viable* alternative to petroleum-driven cars that would cause less pollution.

- NASA decided that the plan to establish a colony on Neptune is not a *viable* one.

(vur choo OH so)	# virtuoso

noun: highly skilled performing artist

adj: exhibiting the masterly techniques of a virtuoso

Picture this:
virtue oh so

This *virtuoso* has a *virtue oh so* rare—
he spreads cheer far and near.

■ Jimi Hendrix was a guitar *virtuoso* who developed a new style of playing that still influences musicians today.

■ It is rare for a person to be a *virtuoso* on more than one musical instrument.

■ Our school's all-state forward delivered a *virtuoso* performance last night, scoring thirty-two points, dishing out eight assists, pulling down twelve rebounds, and forcing six turnovers.

virulent

(VEER yuh lunt)

extremely poisonous;
bitterly hostile

Picture this:
Vye roo* lent

What's wrong with Vye?

She misses her kangaroo. She lent it to a guy named Guy, and it caught a really bad virus and died.

Poor *Vye*. The *roo* she *lent* Guy got
a *virulent* virus and died.

■ The *virulent* computer virus spread very rapidly around
the world through the Internet.

■ Researchers working with *virulent* microorganisms are
required to take many precautions so that the microorganisms
don't leave the laboratory and infect people or animals.

■ The *virulent* criticism of her carefully thought out proposal
angered the governor.

* *Roo* is informal Australian English for kangaroo.

whimsical

unpredictable;
fanciful

Picture this:
whim* sickle

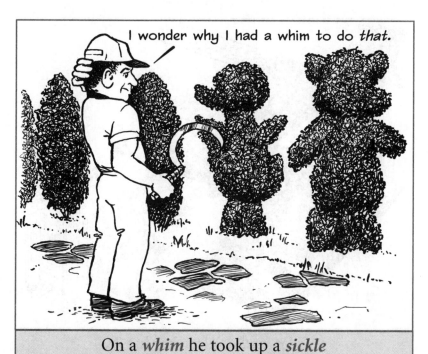

On a *whim* he took up a *sickle*
to create *whimsical* shapes.

■ The movie *The Wizard of Oz* displays a *whimsical* sense
of humor that appeals to both children and adults.

■ When he was feeling *whimsical*, the science fiction writer
Isaac Asimov enjoyed writing limericks—short, humorous,
often nonsensical verse.

■ Sabrina was in one of her *whimsical* moods: "Let's do
something different today," she said to her boyfriend. "Let's
act out a scene from *Romeo and Juliet* in Mr. Harrison's
physics class."

* A *whim* is a capricious desire.

zealot (ZEL ut)

fanatic; person who shows excessive zeal

Picture this:
Z lot

A *Z lot zealot* admiring his Zs.

■ In his book *The True Believer*, Eric Hoffer argued that political *zealots* are often motivated by a need to compensate for a feeling of personal inadequacy.

■ Senator Smith is a *zealot* when it comes to the issue of conservation; she supports far more measures to protect the environment than anyone else in Congress.

■ Uncle Rick could be regarded as a *zealot* when it comes to supporting his political party; he has voted for all the candidates of his party in every election since 1975.

Memory Check 25

Match each word and its link to the corresponding definition.

undermine	vaporize	virulent
1. **under mine** __	2. **vapor eyes** __	3. **Vye roo lent** __
viable	trifling	uniformity
4. **Vye a bull** __	5. **Try Fling** __	6. **uniform at tea** __
turmoil	truncate	virtuoso
7. **term oil** __	8. **trunk Kate** __	9. **virtue oh so** __
unwarranted	whimsical	zealot
10. **a warrant Ted** __	11. **whim sickle** __	12. **Z lot** __

a. shorten
b. weaken
c. fanatic
d. unjustified
e. bitterly hostile
f. practical

g. sameness
h. turn into vapor
i. highly skilled performing artist
j. unimportant
k. fanciful
l. great commotion and confusion

Showtime 25

Fill in the blanks in the following sentences with the word or set of words that best fits the meaning of the sentence as a whole.

1. _____ in the layout of a newspaper makes it easy for readers to locate the type of article they want to read in each issue.
   a. Seclusion   b. Virtuoso   c. Uniformity   d. Tenacity   e. Penury

2. Beth is such a _____ when it comes to supporting her favorite political candidate that she gave up her job to work full time as a volunteer in his campaign.
   a. zealot   b. virtuoso   c. turmoil   d. sycophant   e. sage

3. The editor of the 1,000-page novel decided to _____ it because she felt that a 700-page book would be more popular with readers.
   a. vaporize   b. undermine   c. subside   d. truncate   e. scrutinize

4. The prime minister regarded the statement by the president of the neighboring country that "Any necessary measures would be taken" as _____ to a declaration of war.

    a. virulent   b. tantamount   c. unwarranted   d. trifling   e. viable

5. My English teacher is always reminding the class not to make _____ assumptions in our essays and to make sure that any ideas that we suggest for improving society are _____ .

    a. whimsical.....superficial
    b. trifling.....superfluous
    c. unwarranted.....viable
    d. viable.....undermined
    e. virulent.....unwarranted

6. The success of our group project was _____ by the fact that we could never agree on anything, so there was always _____ in the group.

    a. undermined.....turmoil
    b. vaporized.....uniformity
    c. truncated.....trifling
    d. stupefied.....restraint
    e. scrutinized.....virtuosos

7. Military planners believe that space-based weapons can be developed that will be able to _____ almost instantly _____ targets.

    a. truncate.....viable
    b. repel.....unwarranted
    c. undermine.....whimsical
    d. subside.....trifling
    e. vaporize.....terrestrial

8. Although she was a violin _____ , Alice did make two _____ mistakes in her recital.

    a. zealot.....trifling
    b. sycophant.....unwarranted
    c. turmoil.....superfluous
    d. virtuoso.....trifling
    e. hedonist.....whimsical

ANSWERS

Meet the Stars
MEMORY CHECK
1. d   2. a   3. g   4. e   5. c
6. b   7. f
SHOWTIME
1. e   2. c   3. d   4. e   5. b
6. c   7. b   8. e

Quiz 1
MEMORY CHECK
1. g   2. k   3. h   4. e   5. a
6. f   7. d   8. l   9. j   10. b
11. i   12. c
SHOWTIME
1. b   2. a   3. a   4. c   5. e
6. b   7. b   8. e

Quiz 2
MEMORY CHECK
1. e   2. a   3. c   4. g   5. i
6. d   7. l   8. b   9. j   10. h
11. f   12. k
SHOWTIME
1. b   2. e   3. b   4. d   5. b
6. e   7. d   8. d

Quiz 3
MEMORY CHECK
1. g   2. f   3. d   4. k   5. a
6. h   7. c   8. i   9. l   10. e
11. b   12. j
SHOWTIME
1. b   2. d   3. e   4. b   5. c
6. d   7. e   8. d

Quiz 4
MEMORY CHECK
1. d   2. b   3. f   4. j   5. a
6. c   7. g   8. k   9. e   10. h
11. l   12. i
SHOWTIME
1. b   2. b   3. d   4. b   5. e
6. a   7. c   8. b

Quiz 5
MEMORY CHECK
1. a   2. h   3. l   4. e   5. g
6. k   7. j   8. f   9. c   10. b
11. d   12. i
SHOWTIME
1. d   2. c   3. d   4. d   5. e
6. b   7. c   8. d

Quiz 6
MEMORY CHECK
1. b   2. j   3. a   4. l   5. f
6. h   7. e   8. k   9. i   10. d
11. g   12. c
SHOWTIME
1. c   2. e   3. c   4. a   5. b
6. a   7. e   8. b

Quiz 7
MEMORY CHECK
1. c   2. h   3. g   4. e   5. a
6. d   7. i   8. b   9. k   10. j
11. f   12. l
SHOWTIME
1. e   2. d   3. a   4. e   5. c
6. d   7. b   8. c

Quiz 8
MEMORY CHECK
1. j   2. e   3. d   4. a   5. b
6. f   7. h   8. i   9. l   10. g
11. c   12. k
SHOWTIME
1. b   2. b   3. d   4. a   5. e
6. c   7. b   8. a

Quiz 9
MEMORY CHECK
1. c   2. g   3. f   4. k   5. j
6. e   7. l   8. h   9. b   10. i
11. a   12. d
SHOWTIME
1. a   2. d   3. c   4. e   5. b
6. d   7. c   8. b

Quiz 10
MEMORY CHECK
1. k	2. e	3. h	4. d	5. b
6. f	7. c	8. i	9. a	10. g
11. j	12. l			

SHOWTIME
1. d	2. a	3. b	4. c	5. c
6. a	7. d	8. c		

Quiz 11
MEMORY CHECK
1. d	2. b	3. g	4. a	5. h
6. c	7. e	8. i	9. k	10. j
11. l	12. f			

SHOWTIME
1. c	2. d	3. d	4. a	5. e
6. b	7. a	8. d		

Quiz 12
MEMORY CHECK
1. j	2. f	3. c	4. d	5. h
6. i	7. e	8. g	9. a	10. b
11. k	12. l			

SHOWTIME
1. c	2. a	3. e	4. e	5. b
6. b	7. c	8. d		

Quiz 13
MEMORY CHECK
1. a	2. e	3. l	4. f	5. d
6. c	7. h	8. b	9. i	10. j
11. k	12. g			

SHOWTIME
1. e	2. a	3. d	4. c	5. c
6. b	7. e	8. b		

Quiz 14
MEMORY CHECK
1. a	2. b	3. l	4. f	5. j
6. e	7. h	8. g	9. c	10. d
11. i	12. k			

SHOWTIME
1. d	2. b	3. b	4. e	5. e
6. e	7. e	8. a		

Quiz 15
MEMORY CHECK
1. b	2. d	3. e	4. i	5. c
6. l	7. g	8. k	9. j	10. h
11. a	12. f			

SHOWTIME
1. a	2. b	3. c	4. b	5. e
6. c	7. b	8. e		

Quiz 16
MEMORY CHECK
1. c	2. k	3. a	4. h	5. d
6. e	7. g	8. b	9. j	10. i
11. f	12. l			

SHOWTIME
1. c	2. e	3. a	4. c	5. e
6. d	7. b	8. e		

Quiz 17
MEMORY CHECK
1. j	2. h	3. d	4. i	5. f
6. l	7. g	8. c	9. b	10. k
11. a	12. e			

SHOWTIME
1. d	2. b	3. d	4. e	5. e
6. a	7. b	8. c		

Quiz 18
MEMORY CHECK
1. e	2. l	3. a	4. b	5. f
6. g	7. d	8. h	9. k	10. c
11. j	12. i			

SHOWTIME
1. e	2. e	3. c	4. e	5. d
6. b	7. a	8. b		

Quiz 19
MEMORY CHECK
1. l	2. f	3. k	4. a	5. b
6. d	7. h	8. e	9. j	10. c
11. g	12. i			

SHOWTIME
1. c	2. a	3. a	4. d	5. b
6. c	7. d	8. c		

Quiz 20
MEMORY CHECK

1. b	2. j	3. f	4. c	5. g
6. a	7. d	8. k	9. l	10. e
11. h	12. i			

SHOWTIME

1. e	2. d	3. a	4. e	5. c
6. a	7. d	8. a		

Quiz 21
MEMORY CHECK

1. j	2. a	3. l	4. k	5. c
6. b	7. d	8. f	9. e	10. g
11. h	12. i			

SHOWTIME

1. a	2. b	3. b	4. c	5. b
6. c	7. a	8. c		

Quiz 22
MEMORY CHECK

1. i	2. c	3. a	4. j	5. b
6. f	7. g	8. d	9. e	10. l
11. h	12. k			

SHOWTIME

1. d	2. e	3. a	4. b	5. c
6. e	7. a	8. a		

Quiz 23
MEMORY CHECK

1. h	2. e	3. d	4. f	5. l
6. c	7. g	8. b	9. j	10. a
11. k	12. i			

SHOWTIME

1. e	2. b	3. b	4. c	5. d
6. b	7. a	8. a		

Quiz 24
MEMORY CHECK

1. d	2. j	3. h	4. g	5. e
6. k	7. c	8. l	9. f	10. i
11. b	12. a			

SHOWTIME

1. c	2. b	3. d	4. c	5. e
6. a	7. c	8. a		

Quiz 25
MEMORY CHECK

1. b	2. h	3. e	4. f	5. j
6. g	7. l	8. a	9. i	10. d
11. k	12. c			

SHOWTIME

1. c	2. a	3. d	4. b	5. c
6. a	7. e	8. d